The BBQ
& Campfire
Recipe Book

The BBQ & Campfire Recipe Book

Luke Cox

SUMMERSDALE

Summersdale Publishers Ltd
46 West Street
Chichester
West Sussex
PO19 1RP
UK

www.summersdale.com

Printed and bound in Great Britain.

ISBN 1 84024 244 2

This book is dedicated to everyone at Westbourne Villas for foolishly letting me loose in their kitchen in the first place, and for allowing me to continue once they saw the havoc I could wreak.

My thanks and love to Summerly Devito (for Italian inspiration), Tom 'ah maaan' Sills (for his scary ghost story), and to Liz Kershaw and all at Summersdale.

Contents

Baked Passion Bananas
Chocolate Bananas
Baked Pears
Strawberry Syllabub
Stuffed Blackberry Nectarines
Roasted Honey Peaches
Honey Butter Pineapple
Crumbly Delight

The Devils
Simple Mojito
Cuba Libra
Frozen Margarita
Strawberry Daiquiri
Raspberry Bellini

The Angels
Iced Tea
Strawberry and Banana Smoothie
Kiwi, Grapefruit and Honey Smoothie

About this book

The recipes in this book are designed to be easy to prepare, fun to cook and good to eat. They are designed to demystify the barbecue for the inexperienced, and to allow more experienced chefs to spice up the basic stalwarts of outdoor cooking. They are also designed to give you some ideas and suggestions for when your friends turn up at eleven o'clock with carrier bags full of economy burgers expecting you to whip up something delicious.

Whatever the occasion these recipes should come in handy, even if you're sitting indoors with a troop of sausages and a legion of vegetable kebabs, waiting for the rain to stop, or huddled on the beach round a small disposable grill – and even if you're short of inspiration, remember that good quality ingredients cooked over a fire will nearly always turn out to be tasty: never be afraid to tinker about with the measurements to find out what suits you best. Also remember, more importantly, that – as long as you're safe and sensible – the great outdoors is the most light-hearted cooking stage in the world: it's something anyone can try and everyone can enjoy – and if your favourite recipe crashes and burns there'll always be more sausages to play with. Now get your sun hat on, and get out there and enjoy yourself ...

Beard to Tail: The History of the Barbecue and Campfire in 699 Words

It all began one evening in 1492 when, as we all know, Columbus sailed the Ocean Blue and discovered the New World. During one of his landfalls he discovered something else. On a small island in the West Indies (so named, by Columbus, because he thought he had sailed the whole way round the world and hit India again, the poor dear) he and his men came across a tribe who were all huddled round a smouldering tree. Records are sketchy – and the language barrier must have been quite incredible – but it seems Columbus' crew were able to work out that the locals had buried a whole pig under the tree, which was still smoking after having been hit by lightning and burnt to a crisp the previous day, and were waiting for it to cook. 'Barbacoa!' exclaimed one of Columbus' excited seamen, realising that the cunning locals had found away to cook an entire animal all at once, without having to chop any bits off it.

The Spanish Court, on Christopher's return, were more impressed with his discovery of an entire continent, and as a result his expedition's far more important result – the uncovering of a whole new method of food preparation – went largely unnoticed throughout Europe for many years. However, French traders, moving through the Caribbean towards what are now the southern states of America, heard the legend of the buried pig and took it with them wherever they went, and the preparation of food over or under charcoal became a feature of Haitian and Louisiana cuisine. It was particularly useful for early settlers as it allowed a whole animal to be cooked all at once with little preparation and without the need to build an oven: hence the Spanish sailor's exclamation and the French perversion of it – *barbe à que*, or beard to tail – from which the English word is purportedly derived, and hence its phenomenal following in the USA (from where the acronym BBQ originates – with roadside diners advertising refreshment and pool tables, or Bar, Beer and Cue) and Australia (where the weather is more suited to outdoor cooking). Though through the years the method has changed considerably, we still cook hearty, satisfying food over smouldering bits of burnt tree the world over, and you can tell that to the whole tribe while they huddle round waiting for their sausages.

In the centuries before that fateful lightning strike on an unnamed West Indian island the culinary landscape outside the kitchen was a bleak and featureless tundra. Indeed, in those days there was little to do on a hot summer's evening other than gnaw on a sausage roll and contemplate life's big questions: Why are we here? How do we get back? How can I make my marshmallow more interesting? Until, that is, a group of youngsters, clad in their tribe's traditional green jumpers, peaked caps and woggles, grew tired of listening to the strains of *Thus Spoke Zarathustra* echoing over the hills, took their destinies into their own hands and roasted their fluffy confections on the end of a stick. And Lo! The campfire was born. Of course, cooking over wood fires is as old a trick as humankind – older, even, as there is evidence that our early ancestors, Peking Man, roasted meat in their humble dwellings (although anthropologists are unable to tell us what Peking Woman was doing while this was going on). Nowadays we use the campfire in the absence of other heat sources for warmth and light, and as a backdrop to scary ghost stories – but it is more than that: the campfire represents a return to nature – it is a symbol of our primal instinct and our ability to stave off fearsome predators with our superior intellect. Why else would a supposedly civilised people endure moist socks, the constant threat of spiders lurking in the darkest recess of a sleeping bag and the public spectacle of being unable to correctly assemble a tent? My advice to you: wheel that dusty barbecue out of the shed, don your most battered hiking boots, feel yourself regress to the level of a hulking Neanderthal – and consummate the experience by enjoying some really tasty food.

Getting Started

Barbecues

Barbecue Types

If you don't already have your own barbecue the first thing you'll need to do is get hold of or build one. If buying, invest wisely. You don't need to spend a fortune on something chrome-plated and chic, but it should be sturdy (test it in the shop to see if it wobbles) and made of a material hardy enough to resist the inevitable winter months of neglect without rusting and falling apart. The range in the average hardware, DIY or garden shop is usually immense and bewildering, but there are four basic designs.

1) The Brazier Barbecue

This is by far the most common, the simplest and the cheapest design, and usually consists of a large metal bowl, or sometimes a half-barrel, often with a lid and adjustable grill heights. They are also known as kettle barbecues and are sometimes made from cast iron. A brazier barbecue should be sufficient for most of the recipes listed in this book, and cooking times have been calculated assuming that this is the design you are using (if using other designs the estimated times should not vary considerably, but are likely to be slightly shorter). The principle drawbacks of the brazier are that, as there is no air flowing *through* the coal (only over its surface), in still air the coals can be difficult to get evenly alight, and your food will take longer to cook.

2) The Air-flow Barbecue

This is a slightly more sophisticated design. The bowl

section is usually shallower and flatter and has air vents cut into its underside, with the charcoal resting above on a perforated platform. This means that the air is drawn through the bowl, heated by the charcoal and continues upwards to cook your food. While air-flow barbecues are certainly easier to light they are not necessarily more efficient as they cook faster and have the tendency to sear food without cooking its centre. You should certainly get a model with an adjustable grill – be prepared to raise the grill height if the food cooks too quickly, and to use more charcoal than you would if using a brazier. That said, an air-flow barbecue is more reliable on a still day and will allow even cooking across a larger surface – one of these is therefore a serious consideration if cooking for more than four people, and if you are at all an impatient person, I'd say it's worth shelling out the extra money.

3) The Gas Powered Barbecue

Gas barbecues are usually the most expensive sort, are generally the most reliable and are certainly the least fun. They differ from conventional indoor gas grills in that the flaming gas heats 'lava' rocks (usually of an artificial or ceramic material), and it is these that heat your food. They have an advantage over other designs in that they are relatively quick to heat up and are more or less impervious to most adverse weather conditions (you could even cook with one in light rain, although I don't see why you'd want to). They have adjustable temperature controls, and some of the flashier models have integral hotplates for keeping cooked food warm. You are also able to dispense with the tiresome rigmarole of lighting and handling charcoal, getting your clothes smoky and so forth. Unfortunately, the food cooked on them often tastes much like it would if you'd simply shoved it under the grill indoors, the lava rocks making for a poor charcoal substitute, and this seems to defeat the point a little, but if you are attempting to feed the Five Thousand, or if you want to be the envy of your neighbours, then they are definitely worth considering. Buy one that can also be lit manually (piezo-electric sparking devices are the first thing to break on any range, and they won't work if wet), and opt for the most idiot-proof control system you can find to reduce needless fiddling with knobs whilst cooking.

4) The Disposable Barbecue

Most disposable barbecues I've come across consist of an aluminium tray filled with charcoal, with a perforated metal lid (which serves as the grill) resting over an internal piece of touch paper. These are a brilliant invention for those of us without gardens wanting a barbecue in the park or on the beach, or for impromptu gatherings. They are cheap (you can usually get them in pound shops or thrift stores) and generally reliable. The one thing I would say about disposable barbecues is that they never last quite as long as you'd hoped or were informed they would, mainly because the charcoal used is cheap and burns quickly, so cook only simple recipes on them, and make sure you buy one more tray than you thought you'd need. If I'm wrong then you can always save it for another time.

Building your own Barbecue

Some do-it-yourself is the other option you might consider, and this is certainly worthwhile if you have your own garden, you enjoy cooking outdoors, and you're not moving anywhere for a little while. If you have no bricklaying experience you can build a sturdy barbecue without mortar with far less hassle than you'd first imagine. Try the method below, or consult a specialist DIY book for further advice and more complicated designs.

Mortarless Brick Barbecue
Size 110 cm x 86 cm x 80 cm (43" x 34" x 32")

This design stands under waist height (80 cm / 32"), has two grills for cooking at different speeds, and has a useful surface for resting dishes and utensils on while you cook.

250 standard bricks (includes 9 extra bricks to allow for breakages)
2 metal kitchen grills of 60 cm x 40 cm (24" x 16")
a level spot at least 130 cm x 100 cm (51" x 39")
chalk
heavy hammer
tape measure

Measure and mark out with chalk a rectangle on even ground 110 cm x 86 cm (43" x 34"). It is important that this area should be level as there is no mortar – or cement – to support the bricks. Concrete is the best surface to build on; the next best is a patio. Ensure that this rectangle is positioned well away from overhanging trees or bushes (or cut them back). Also ensure that one of longest sides to the rectangle is the most accessible, as this is where the grill opening will be.

Following your lines, build a flat rectangle of bricks inside the chalked area. Do this by starting in one corner and laying two bricks next to each other to form a square. Lay two bricks next to that with their longest sides abutting the first bricks. Continue until you've filled the rectangle to close any gaps, and gently tap in the sides with a hammer.

Build another course (layer) on top, so that the directions of the two-brick squares oppose those of the bricks beneath them. This time do not completely fill in the rectangle. Instead leave a space two bricks wide on the longest side, and three bricks long on the shorter for the firebox. The second course will therefore have a rectangle 'cut' into it, walled on three sides, open where it juts into the longer side of the barbecue at its front. Again, gently straighten the bricks with a hammer.

Continue building courses in the same manner as the second course until you have a brick frame eight courses high. Carefully push the bricks whose wythes (shorter sides) face the firebox (the rectangular space) so they jut out into the firebox by about 5 cm / 2" on the fourth and seventh courses. These bricks will support your grills. Line the base of the firebox with kitchen foil and you're ready to lay and light the fire.

Charcoal

With the basics sorted, the next thing you'll need is something to power your barbecue. If you're using a gas-powered barbecue you should refer to the manufacturer's instructions as to what sort of gas you should be using and where to buy it. If you're using a disposable barbecue the problem is already solved as the charcoal is part of the package. For the rest of us the answer is on sale in most petrol station forecourts, and you will have a choice between the two forms in which charcoal is usually sold (alternatively dry wood can be used, but it is much harder to light and most brazier-type barbecues are not really designed for it). Both types of fuel are made by heating wood at high temperatures in the absence of oxygen, leaving only the friable carbon residue behind – and this burns at a higher temperature than the wood itself as it is a purer fuel.

1) Briquettes

These are the pleasingly ovoid, pre-processed charcoal

blocks most commonly used as barbecue fuel. They are inexpensive and widely available in large bags big enough to fuel a barbecue or three. Store any fuel you have left over in a dry place and you can use it again the next time you cook. Briquettes usually cost a little more than loose charcoal, and can be harder to light, but they do tend to last longer and are less messy to handle. It is now also possible to buy self-lighting briquettes, and although these are more expensive you may be tempted to opt for them to make life that little bit easier.

2) Lumpwood

These brittle, irregular, unprocessed fragments of charcoal are dustier than briquettes, but lumpwood is cheaper and always seems to be easier to light. As it is less dense, lumpwood will burn faster than a similar volume of briquettes, so make sure that you buy plenty.

From a purely environmental perspective, I would recommend lumpwood over briquettes if you can find some produced domestically: 97 per cent of charcoal used comes from the Mangrove forests of Indonesia and has contributed to their massive depletion. Smaller charcoal ovens in the West usually use wood from sustainable ecosystems. If you are at all concerned about the future of the planet then check the packaging carefully to see from where your charcoal originates.

Laying the Fire

The next stage is putting the charcoal into the barbecue bowl. My advice would be to line the bowl or firebox first with kitchen foil (with its most reflective side facing up) if using a brazier or self-built barbecue. Not only will this make your barbecue more efficient, reflecting the heat from the charcoal upwards, but it will make it easier to clean out at the end of the day. Lay the charcoal evenly so that it extends right to the edges of the cooking area, and ensure the depth is consistent. If using lumpwood a depth of 8 cm / 3" is sufficient, while the layer should not be more than three coals deep if using briquettes.

Lighting the Barbecue
It is the lighting of the charcoal that most people perceive as requiring special technical expertise and a Y chromosome. It can, admittedly, be infuriating in the wrong weather conditions or with the wrong equipment, but if you are prepared and persevere it should not present you with too many difficulties.

1) **Position your barbecue out of the wind** (although a little breeze is okay, and can help as it fans the flames. Too much wind and you'll have difficulty lighting a match). Also, remember to remove the grill as it will restrict access to lighting the fuel.

2) **Heap the charcoal into a pyramid in the centre of the cooking area.** You should first lay the fire, as described above, to check you have enough charcoal.

3) **Sprinkle barbecue lighter fluid evenly over the charcoal, or break barbecue lighter blocks into small pieces and distribute them evenly amongst and under the coals.** Do not use lighter fluid intended for a different purpose, and under no circumstances use petrol or a similar accelerant.

4) **If using lighter fluid, allow 15 seconds for the fluid to absorb into the charcoal.** (Skip this stage if using lighter blocks.)

5) **Light the charcoal or lighter blocks using a long cook's match or taper.** Do not use a cigarette lighter as you will end up burning your hands. Light the coals evenly.

6) **Carefully spread the charcoal over the cooking area.** Do this using a pair of tongs until the charcoal is spread to an even depth.

7) **Allow the charcoal to become evenly alight before you cook over it.** You should replace the grill now, but it can be anything up to 30 minutes before the charcoal is entirely alight. This seems a frustrating length of time but there's no point cooking over the charcoal until it is up to temperature. It will be ready when all the coals develop a white colouring (which is ash forming on the outer layer). At night it is much easier to tell as the flames recede and the coals begin to glow a lobster pink.

The temperature your barbecue cooks at will be dependent on the weather conditions (mainly the breeze) and the height your grill rests above the coals. You must simply use your common sense to move the grill upwards if your food cooks too quickly.

If you need to add more charcoal to continue cooking, e.g. for a dessert, it will light itself if added to already-glowing embers. Make sure it is fully and evenly alight, as in the steps above, before you continue to cook.

8) **If your barbecue will not light properly,** carefully remove the charcoal, wearing oven gloves and using tongs, and place it in a metal bucket. Repeat steps 3-5 and return the coals to the barbecue bowl, spreading them out evenly as before.

Cooking on the Barbecue

This is not rocket science as long as you keep things simple. Barbecues often come with lids, and these are handy in stiff breezes, but try to resist the temptation to roast massive joints of meat under there. Personally, I think it rather a waste of time as barbecues have a tendency to sear meat, leading to awfully long cooking times for larger cuts. Instead, treat the barbecue as a grill with a smoky flavour and you won't go too wrong, and use it to its strengths.

So, marinate fish and meat so the outside can develop a crisp husk while the inside remains moist with the flavours absorbed, cook fish and vegetables in foil to seal in their juiciness, and bake fruit so it turns into a delicious, irresistible mush. The trickiest thing you'll have to do is allow enough time for meat to be properly marinated, allowing all the juices to permeate it. I advise two hours for meat and poultry, and fish – which is often tasty with as little as possible added – needs a shorter time, between 30 minutes and 1 hour. It'll never get more complicated than that, I promise. For simplicity's sake, assume when following the recipes that when you come to cook your coals are hot and your grill is adjusted to a medium height, always stay safe, check your food is properly cooked before you eat it, and you should have a happy and hitch-free time.

Cleaning and Oiling

Opinion is divided as to whether, to stop the two sticking together, one should oil the grill or the food. I would suggest the latter is the more sensible, especially as you may be using oil within a marinade or baste. Inevitably there will be a degree of sticky residue left on the grill, especially from the meat as it chars. This can be reduced by allowing meat to sear fully before it is turned over – i.e.

rather than turning constantly, allow one side to cook fully, then turn.

Between courses you should certainly scrape the worst of the mess off the grill. It would be a shame to spoil a delicate fish dish with the thick taste of beef, for instance. If cooking both at the same time allow them separate spaces on the grill, and certainly keep dishes prepared specifically for vegetarians away from meaty tastes. Otherwise, remove the grill with an oven-gloved hand and allow it to cool for a minute or two. While it is still warm, carefully scrape off the larger bits of residue with a metal spatula, and remove the rest with a metal scourer or wire brush.

Special Equipment

Beyond that usually found in a kitchen there are only a few things you'll need:

A good set of metal tongs with rubber or plastic handles – you don't want to prick the food and let all the delicious juices come spurting out, but quite aside from that they're the easiest thing to use as they keep your hands a safe distance away from the heat.

A good metal spatula or fish slice – you'll need this for turning fish over, obviously, and for burgers. It also comes in handy for scraping off any large bit of food stuck to the grill.

A brush for basting – this will prove useful for many barbecue recipes which require the food to be kept well oiled and moist. The recipes in this book adhere to the principle that it is the *food* that should be oiled, not the grill, in order to prevent it sticking. Use a brush with natural bristles (and not a used paintbrush).

A set of 4 flat metal skewers, which experience will teach you are easier to use for cooking kebabs as the food does not turn around upon them. These are not essential and bamboo skewers will do just as well if you're on a budget, but they will save a lot of hassle soaking the wooden skewers in water to stop them burning. Metal skewers are also useful for testing meat is properly done.

A big roll of kitchen foil – this is something that both barbecue and campfire cooking can use an awful lot of. When wrapping food in it ready to be cooked, bear in mind that you want to keep the heat *in*, so use some common sense and keep the shiniest side innermost.

A wire brush or a metal scourer – essential for cleaning the barbecue grill.

A jug of water – keep this handy near the barbecue. The fat dripping from meat onto the coals can cause small flare-ups, which can be extinguished with a fingertip-flick of water.

Campfires

Campfire food will usually have a greater element of pragmatism about it, as you are less likely to have access to all the things you want. If we're talking about the true outdoor experience – i.e. just you, your knapsack on your back and no opportunity to wash for four or five days, then I really can't help you, and trust me you need help. However, assuming you are not disappearing off into the dark unknown to survive on just a couple of tins of beans, that you have access to running water, somewhere to prepare food either beforehand or at the site, and the materials for building a decent campfire, then most of the recipes in this book should prove useful. Some will appear impractical, and I would agree that when cooking on a campfire your recipes should be kept as simple as possible. However, the advantage you will have over the barbecue is the ability to prepare a wide range of dishes, staples and sauces in pots and pans there and then, over the fire. Other recipes have been designed with the campfire in mind, and there really is no easier way to cook than to wrap something in foil and place it in a campfire's glowing embers.

Building a Campfire

If doing this purely for the purposes of cooking (as opposed to just light and warmth) bear in mind the same principles as barbecues. Unless the food is encased in foil treat the fire like a grill, so you will need something to support the food above the heat source. The best way I've found to do this is to take along with you the grill rack from an oven or barbecue – especially if you are walking or travelling by car to your destination and space is not at a premium. This can then be propped up on bricks or rocks above raked, glowing embers to provide a good-sized grilling space.

Organised or official campsites may provide campfire spaces near your pitch – often a circle made of breeze blocks, sometimes with a grill – and a supply of forklift palettes that can be chopped for firewood. Elsewhere you will have to improvise. The important rules are that your wood should be dead (and not green – living wood burns badly) and preferably dry, and that your fire should be constructed in a manner that allows decent airflow through it. The design to avoid involves large logs balanced against each other like guns before a Napoleonic battle, or a Native American tepee – the logs will collapse in on themselves as they burn, killing the fire. Instead, form a square on the ground from larger pieces of wood. Use two logs to form two sides on the bottom, two logs on top placed overlapping the edges of these, and at right angles to form the other two sides, and so on. You will find this an easy design to make if you are using palette wood. Stuff the laid fire loosely with kindling and then smaller twigs and branches on top. The best kindling is dry, screwed up newspaper. Otherwise use a small knife to make wood shavings, or collect dead leaves and bracken.

Lighting the Fire
As with barbecues this can sometimes be a testing experience. Never use petrol, no matter how tempting. Use cook's matches, a taper or a ball of paper on the end of a stick to light the kindling. Alternatively, as many regular campers will testify, a handheld gas torch is a wise investment and will remove most of your worries.

Once the fire is going, wait until the larger pieces of wood have collapsed down into embers. Using a stick, rake the embers flat and carefully position your grill above them so it is about 14 cm / 5" from the heat, raking more embers into the space under the grill if it becomes too cool.

Campfire Cooking

The principles of campfire cooking, for the purposes of this book at least, are largely similar to those of the barbecue. Food can be grilled, wrapped in foil and placed into the embers, or fried and boiled in conventional frying- and saucepans. There is little point messing around with the more sophisticated equipment on the market, such as Dutch ovens and so forth, which will inevitably give you a headache because of their complexity, though there are numerous specialist societies devoted to these if you wish to experiment. For the time being *keep it simple*, and use your imagination in adapting the recipes here to what you have available. For example, use sealable freezer bags to transport or prepare marinades: you don't always *need* a 'shallow dish'. The basic basics of what you'll need to cook outdoors (i.e. away from the immediate vicinity of a well stocked kitchen, so this goes for beach barbecues too) are as follows:

A big box of matches, ideally cook's matches (the long ones)

A grilling tray stolen from your oven will do

One large and one small sharp knife, one 18 cm / 7" and one 8 cm / 3" blade

A chopping board – heavy, sturdy, wooden

A medium pan with lid, preferably heavy-based

Rubber handled metal tongs and fish slice for turning your food

Natural-bristle brush for basting

A frying pan – avoid metal handles

A wooden spoon

A colander

A jug – preferably with measuring capability

Cutlery – essential: cutting things with plastic is no fun

Crockery – less so: to avoid washing up use paper plates, bread and buns

A serving spoon

A scary ghost story. How about the one about the cat with human hands – it steals different parts of different people until it becomes entirely human ...

Napkins or a roll of kitchen towel

Plenty of water – in bottles; even if you have access to drinking water it's a good idea to have something to transport it in from the tap

Kitchen foil and resealable plastic bags

Metal scourer or wire brush for cleaning the grill

A bin bag – respect your environment and take your rubbish away with you

Safe and Healthy Eating

Barbecue and Campfire Safety

However much fun a barbecue is, it is vital to remember that the cooking platform is essentially a metal bucket filled with very hot coals, or in the case of campfires, a heap of burning wood. Add to this children running around in the immediate vicinity, season with a smattering of merry and possibly drunken adults, and you have a recipe for an extremely unpleasant experience indeed. To avoid a trip to the burns unit of your local hospital it is necessary that you take responsibility for the following:

Ensuring your barbecue is stable. Test it both with and without coals before you light it. Is it likely to fall over? Have the legs been adjusted properly? Is the ground underneath it flat and even? Rectify any faults before you light the coals, and if you can't, then DON'T USE IT.

Positioning your barbecue or campfire safely. Think where your guests and family will be. Identify the routes they'll use in and out of the house or to and from toilets, and where you'll be serving the food. You should ideally have a separate serving area (a table, for instance, set away from the barbecue itself) so you don't have hordes of people crowded around while you cook. Try and position your barbecue or campfire so it is in a place people will not be constantly walking past. DO NOT position it next to a door, on a slope or steps, or on uneven ground. Check that the immediate area is free from debris over which people could trip and fall.

Avoiding fires. Consider your immediate environment. Is there anything close to the barbecue that could easily burn?

Remember that sparks from barbecues and campfires, or 'flare-ups' while you're cooking, could ignite nearby paper, wood, fabric etc. Try and leave a gap of at least three feet between the fire or barbecue and flammable materials, i.e. sheds and fences, and do not position your barbecue or fire under overhanging trees. Move any fuel sources, lighter fuels etc. well away from the cooking area when you've finished using them, and check that any other potential fire hazards (e.g. petrol cans, tins of paint, firewood) have been stored somewhere safe. Finally, have a bucket of water handy, just in case.

Lighting the fire safely. Only use accelerants specifically designed for use on a barbecue. If using a fluid ensure that it has been soaked up by the charcoal before lighting. NEVER use petrol to light charcoal or wood. Ignite the charcoal or kindling using cook's matches or a taper. DO NOT add lighter fluid to an already-lit barbecue.

Keeping the barbecue or campfire attended to. While cooking make sure there is always someone looking after the barbecue or attending to the fire. The fat from cooking meat can cause small fires and someone should always be on hand to douse these as they begin. If you have to go elsewhere designate someone as chief food-turner and fire-douser. While eating it may be the case that you have to leave the barbecue unattended, but keep a watchful eye on it, especially if there are children present. Use common sense to keep them out of harm's way.

Putting out the barbecue or campfire. Never try to move the barbecue while the coals and ashes are still hot – and they will remain so for several hours after cooking. If it can be done so in safety, after the barbecue has died right down, leave it where it is and throw the coals away in the morning. Otherwise douse the coals in water until they are covered and leave them for at least half an hour before disposing of them. You might like to add the residue to a compost or to plant beds as it makes a good fertiliser. DO NOT leave hot, disposable barbecues behind on, say, the beach, or cover them with sand. When they are cool take them with you and dispose of them with all your other litter. Equally, DO NOT walk away from a smouldering campfire – douse it well with water.

Food Health and Hygiene

There's no worse *faux pas* than inadvertently poisoning your friends and family. When cooking outdoors the usual rules of food hygiene apply, but it is always worth being extra-vigilant. For a comprehensive guide to safe eating read the latest edition of *Essential Food Hygiene*, published by the Royal Society of Health, and adhere carefully to the dos and don'ts listed below:

DO wash your hands before preparing any sort of food and after any kind of contact with raw meats.

DO check that meat is thoroughly cooked. Reformed meats (e.g. burgers and sausages) and chicken should be cooked all the way through – check with a skewer that the juices of chicken run clear and that no pink colour remains in the centre of burgers and sausages. Cuts of red meat should have no trace of pink remaining on the outside surface.

DON'T use the same utensils for preparing meat and vegetables. **ALWAYS** use separate chopping boards, knives, tongs etc. for preparing and cooking meat.

DO check the use-by dates on pre-packaged products, and especially meat. **DON'T** use any product that has gone past the printed date or has been incorrectly stored. **DO** refrigerate food. Leave as short an interval as possible between removing food from the fridge and cooking or serving it. **DO** use a cool box if transporting food. Prepare foods indoors where possible.

DON'T leave salads, dips etc. uncovered in the kitchen or outdoors. Keep them covered (e.g. with cling film) until they're ready to be served. Be especially careful with salads and other food that will be served raw – prepare them well away from any meat products, cooked or otherwise. **DON'T** use meat marinades as sauces unless they have been boiled though for at least 3 minutes. **DON'T** baste meats with their marinades for the last 3 minutes of the specified cooking time.

DO buy meats with lower fat contents (e.g. fish and poultry, or lean cuts of beef and lamb, with fat trimmed away where possible). **DO** eat plenty of salads, fruit and vegetables!

Conversion Chart and a Note about Weights, Measures and Cooking times

Where possible I've tried to include both imperial and metric measurements where quantities are specified, and of course the conversions are approximate. Generally for herbs, spices, oils, sauces and condiments, the measurements are in teaspoons or tablespoons and are designed to denote just that, rather than acutely specific volumes. The point is that barbecue and campfire cooking are one part science to three parts art to five parts sheer trial and error, so I'd use the recipes as a guide rather than the law. I don't think there's a single recipe here that will be entirely ruined by an overzealous application of paprika or the gratuitous omission of salt – in fact, it's possible they might be improved by it so experiment away, and when you do make a 'mistake' or defining discovery *pretend it's what you intended all along*. It works for me, anyway.

Nevertheless it is always helpful to have a chart handy for approximate conversions between metric and imperial measurements, so here it is:

Metric	Imperial
25 g	1 oz
50 g	2 oz
75 g	3 oz
100 g	4 oz
150 g	6 oz
225 g	8 oz
500 g / 0.5 kg	1 lb
150 ml	¼ pint
300 ml	½ pint
600 ml	1 pint
1 litre / 1000 ml	2 pints

The cooking times, stated at the start of each recipe, refer to the length of time the dishes will take to cook over charcoal or embers, and do not include preparation times for chopping, mixing, parboiling and marinating. They are also provided as a guide rather than a rule: they will vary according to the weather (the temperature of your fire will be higher in a little breeze), the type of barbecue you are using, and the height of the grill above the heat source. Be prepared to raise the grill height if food seems to be cooking too quickly (or lower the temperature on a gas grill), or to extend the cooking period where food is cooking too slowly. Always be sensible and test food with a skewer to make sure it is properly cooked, and never serve undercooked meat. To help ensure this the cooking times tend to err on the side of caution: slightly overcooked meat, which may otherwise cause murmurs of disapproval around a dinner table, is almost expected at a barbecue or campfire, and is infinitely preferable to it being served dangerously underdone.

A Word About the Weather

The unwritten law of outdoor cooking is that the longer and more thorough your preparations, the greater the chance of it all being scuppered by an unexpected downpour. Do peruse the weather reports and pick nice days for your barbecues and camping trips – the ideal conditions you'll be looking for are clear days with a little breeze – but as we all know they are not one hundred per cent reliable. If it does rain whilst barbecuing, get everything inside as quickly as you can and put the charcoal out by dousing it in water before you leave it unattended. Don't be disheartened, for all is not lost – all the recipes here will cook just as well using conventional methods, either under a grill at a medium-high heat, or in an oven pre-heated to 200°C / 400°F. You will lose the characteristic smoky flavour, but this will be a small price to pay for appeasing your hungry guests. If you experience adverse weather whilst camping you are likely to have far less fun as it is difficult (and dangerous) to cook in a tent. Bring inside or cover any unburnt dry wood you have collected, fall back on the recipes that do not require heating, break out the reserve supply of chocolate, and have a pack of cards close to hand whilst you sit out the deluge.

Marinades, Bastes, Rubs, Glazes and Salsas

You can bring out the best in your food by flavouring it either before, during or after it cooks. These simple preparation methods, with which you can experiment to your heart's content, will liven up even the blandest of burgers.

Marinades

These are any combination of flavours, usually in an oil or vinegar-based fluid, in which meat, fish or vegetables rest before cooking. A marinade's effectiveness largely depends on the texture of the food being cooked. Fish, which usually has a light texture, will absorb flavours more quickly than chicken and pork, while beef, with its rich flesh, will resist all but the strongest flavours. Marinades are used heavily in barbecue and campfire cooking and are easy to experiment with. Simply add your favourite herbs and spices to a mixture of olive oil and lemon juice (for a heavy marinade) or white wine vinegar (for a lighter, sharper flavour) and pour it over meat, fish or vegetables in a shallow dish. Three parts olive oil to one part lemon juice will make a simple base for a marinade, but virtually any liquid can be used – I recommend vigorous and wholly unscientific experimentation with pineapple juice (deliciously sweet), any half-finished bottle of wine you have to hand, and of course Worcester and soy sauces.

Allow plenty of time for the food to absorb the flavours of the marinade before it cooks, e.g.:

at least 30 minutes for fish and shellfish
at least 2 hours for chicken, pork and vegetables
at least 4 hours for lamb
at least 6 hours for beef

Remember that the longer you leave the food in the marinade the better it will absorb the flavour, so the preferable thing to do is to marinate in a shallow dish, cover the food and chill it in a fridge overnight.

Bastes

These follow the same principles as marinades, but work on the principle that if you're really pushed for time you can dispense with allowing meat to rest in the sauce and can instead smear it over the food with a brush while it cooks. The flavour won't penetrate meat as well but should crisp to a tasty husk.

Remember, if using leftover marinade as a baste to either boil the sauce through for 3 minutes beforehand, or do not apply the baste for the last 3 minutes of the cooking time.

Rubs

A rub is a simple way to prepare meat prior to cooking and is perfect for when you have little preparation time available. Simply grind or mix together your favourite spices and dried herbs and, as you might expect, rub the mixture into the flesh of the meat you're about to grill. Excellent combinations are thyme, brown sugar, cayenne pepper and a pinch of nutmeg for an instant Caribbean flavour, or garam masala, paprika and chilli powder for a quick Tandoori taste.

Glazes

Anything sticky and edible brushed onto the outside of your food either before or while it cooks will crisp up over heat, and as well as being tasty will make your food glistening and tempting. A glaze will also help to seal in the flavour and stop those delicious juices escaping onto the fire. Experiment with brown sugar and mustard, honey, and fruit chutneys.

Salsas

'Salsa' simply means 'sauce' – it's easy to invigorate the most basic of dishes with one that can be whizzed together in a few seconds flat. Try chopped, roasted peppers, seasoning and a handful of fresh, torn basil leaves, or fresh chopped tomatoes and a selection of your favourite fresh herbs. Spoon the mixture over meat or vegetables fresh from the grill or fire.

Starters

Starters are a remarkably important component of a successful barbecue meal. This is mainly because barbecues require loving care and, above all, time, so you will need something to occupy your guests while your coals get up to a suitable cooking colour (which will invariably take longer than you initially expected). Finger food is a must as it will prepare everyone for the nature of the feast ahead without overfilling their bellies, so you should ideally present an array of tasty dips with crusty bread, tortilla chips, crisps and crudités (slices of fruit and vegetables to use for dipping) alongside tiny delicious morsels designed to whet the appetite. Some of the recipes here – such as the Brie Fondue – do require cooking and so may be best left to the more confident, but there's no reason why they can't be cooked indoors or simply presented later, during the meal. The most important trick to remember with starters is to have them prepared well in advance, leaving you time to cook the rest of the food in earnest.

Cheese and Chive Dip

Serves 4

This is a simple, creamy and tasty dip, certain to whet the appetite. Serve with plenty of cucumber, celery and carrot batons, or simply smeared upon crusty bread.

1 small garlic clove, crushed (optional)
4 oz / 100 g fromage frais
4 oz / 100 g blue cheese (e.g. Dolcelatte)
juice of 1 lemon
2 tablespoons chives, chopped
1 teaspoon chives, chopped, to serve
freshly ground black pepper

In a bowl, beat together the cheese, fromage frais and, if you want an extra tang, the garlic. Add the lemon juice, chives and a liberal sprinkling of black pepper. Spoon the dip out into a serving bowl and serve with a selection of vegetable batons – crunchy celery and cooling cucumber work best.

Brie Fondue

Serves 4-6

This makes a delicious and irresistible centrepiece to any table.

1 whole Brie
sliced apples, carrots or crusty bread to serve

Simply wrap the whole Brie, with rind intact, in kitchen foil and place on the grill for 20-30 minutes, turning it occasionally – or, if serving as an after dinner treat, put the foil parcel directly into the embers and cook for 15-20 minutes.

To serve, unwrap carefully and place on a plate surrounded by apple and carrot crudités, cutting a hole in the top of the Brie to allow access to the soft, squishy cheese inside. For truly messy fun leave some spoons in the Brie and allow your guests to help themselves, spooning it onto crusty French bread.

Rough Cut Guacamole

Serves 4-6

The classic avocado dip needs little introduction. This recipe includes red onion to give the guacamole a rougher texture, but for a smoother paste leave it out or blend all the ingredients in a food processor. Simply serve with tortilla chips, and don't expect any leftovers.

3 ripe avocados
half a red onion, finely chopped
1 small green chilli, deseeded and finely chopped
1 dash Tabasco sauce
1 large garlic clove, crushed
juice of 1 lime
2 tablespoons fresh coriander, roughly chopped
paprika and lime wedges to serve

Halve the avocados, remove the stones and scoop the flesh out into a bowl. Mix in the chilli, lime juice and Tabasco and mash with a fork until smooth. Roughen the mixture by adding the onion, stir well and refrigerate for 1 hour. Before serving stir in the coriander and garnish with a pinch of paprika and lime wedges.

Fat Free Guacamole

Serves 4-6

Using peas instead of avocado, and serving sliced carrots, celery, apples and pears instead of tortilla chips will appease the weight-conscious: most people won't be able to tell the difference ...

10 oz / 350 g defrosted frozen peas
1 salad onion, chopped
1 dash of Tabasco sauce
1 large garlic clove
1 tablespoon reduced fat mayonnaise
½ teaspoon cumin
2 tablespoons fresh coriander, roughly chopped
paprika and lime wedges to serve

Combine all the ingredients except for the coriander and blend in a food processor until of a smooth and even consistency. Ideally, you should refrigerate the mixture for 1 hour. Before serving stir in the coriander, then transfer to a bowl, garnish with lime wedges and a pinch of paprika, and accompany with batons of apple, pear, celery and carrots.

Tomato Salsa

Serves 4-6

Another spicy Mexican classic. An ideal accompaniment to guacamole, best served with tortilla chips, and a superb starter for meat and poultry dishes.

14 oz / 400 g vine tomatoes
½ red onion, chopped
1 green chilli, deseeded and chopped
1 dash Tabasco sauce
juice of 2 limes
2 tablespoons fresh coriander, roughly chopped

Skin the tomatoes by standing them in freshly boiled water for 5 minutes: after this the skins should simply peel off with little effort. Cut out the small hard area at the top of each tomato where it was joined to the vine. Chop and mash the tomatoes, and sieve away any excess clear liquid. In a bowl combine the tomato pulp with the onion, chilli, Tabasco and lime juice and stir well. Refrigerate the mixture for at least one hour, and just before serving stir in the coriander.

Classic Nachos

Serves 4-6

The staple starter of pub menus up and down the country, cheesy nachos are a treat loved by all, and make superbly messy finger food fit for any gathering.

large bag of tortilla chips
1 serving of Rough Cut Guacamole (see page 46)
1 serving of Tomato Salsa (see page 48)
200 ml sour cream
6 oz / 150 g medium Cheddar cheese, grated

Pour the tortilla chips out onto a large microwave or ovenproof dish and heap generous dollops of guacamole and tomato salsa over them. Spoon the sour cream over the sauces and top with the grated cheese. Cook in the microwave for 2 minutes on full power (or until the cheese has melted and bubbles slightly), or in an oven preheated to 220°C / 430°F for 10 minutes. Serve immediately and watch everyone dig in.

Campfire Corn

Serves 1

We'll take a closer look at corn later on: it can take a notoriously long time to cook, but not with this simple method which is perfect for a campfire starter.

1 whole cob of sweet corn
1 lemon
freshly ground black pepper

Remove the corn's outer husk (if necessary) and make a hole in one end with a skewer. Force it onto the end of a long-ish stick and hold the corn directly over the campfire *flames* (be sure to do this at arm's length). When the corn's yellow has turned to a crispy dark brown remove it from the flames, slice the lemon in half and squeeze the juice over the corn. Sprinkle well with freshly ground black pepper and eat immediately.

Baba Ganoush

Serves 4

This delightfully smooth and tasty aubergine dip can be prepared the morning before or a day in advance.

2 aubergines
3 tablespoons lemon juice
1 teaspoon salt
2 large cloves of garlic, crushed
3 tablespoons sour cream
3 tablespoons fresh parsley, chopped
2 tablespoons toasted pine nuts
1 tablespoon olive oil to serve

Prick the aubergines all over with a fork and bake them whole in an oven preheated to 200°C / 400°F for 30 minutes. Remove the aubergines, halve them and scoop out the flesh. Mix with the lemon juice (ideally in a food processor, but if you don't have one a bowl and fork will do) until smooth. Mash together the salt and garlic and add this and the sour cream to the mix. Allow the mixture to cool before stirring in the parsley and pine nuts, then refrigerate until you need to serve it. Just before serving, drizzle the olive oil over the top. An ideal dip for tortilla chips or briefly barbecued pitta bread.

Venetian Cipolline

Serves 6-8

A speciality of Venice, the salty fish and the pickled onions complement each other beautifully, and are certain to leave your guests clamouring for more. Wash down with liberal quantities of Frascati for a truly Italian starter.

2 tins / 100 g of anchovy fillets in oil
1 jar of small pickled silverskin onions
cocktail sticks to serve

Drain both the onions and the anchovies from their liquids. Form parcels by wrapping the flattened fillets around the onions, securing each with a cocktail stick, and serve.

Roasted Marinated Goats' Cheese

Serves 8

Goats' cheese is wonderful because it absorbs flavour so well. These marinated cheeses can be kept for up to two weeks in jam jars and can be brought out and roasted for any occasion, but they work especially well if served just before a barbecue feast.

4 whole goats' cheeses
10 tablespoons olive oil
2 bay leaves
2 teaspoons dried rosemary
3 teaspoons dried thyme
4 unpeeled garlic cloves
2 teaspoons lemon zest
6 whole black peppercorns
2 clean jam jars

A few days in advance, heat the oil in a saucepan over a low heat together with the herbs, bay leaves, garlic, lemon and peppercorns. Infuse (i.e. very gently cook) the mixture for 15-20 minutes, by which time the aroma should be delightful. Meanwhile, place the goats' cheeses in two clean jam jars (two to a jar: it will be worth checking beforehand that the cheeses will fit inside, so use the jars with the widest mouths possible and well-fitting lids). Pour the contents of the saucepan over the cheeses, dividing it equally between the two jars. Screw the lids on tightly and leave them at the top of a fridge for a couple of days.

To cook, remove the cheeses from their jars with a slotted spoon and wrap them individually in foil. Place the parcels on the barbecue grill over hot coals for 25 minutes, by which time the skin should be slightly crusty and the inside deliciously soft. Serve, as with the Brie Fondue, with vegetable crudités.

Crab and Mango Mayonnaise

Serves 4

This exotic yet easy-to-prepare dip is especially recommended as a starter to fish and seafood dishes, but will impress and please on any occasion.

4 oz / 100 g canned crabmeat
3 oz / 75 g ripe mango
2 tablespoons mayonnaise
1 small red chilli, deseeded and finely chopped
2 salad onions, chopped
3 tablespoons lemon juice
8 large basil leaves
2 cucumbers cut into batons, to serve

Peel and finely chop the mango, which if ripe enough should have a soft and slightly stringy consistency, and combine it in a bowl with the chilli, salad onions, lemon juice and mayonnaise. Finally, add the cooked crabmeat, stir well and refrigerate until needed. Just before serving stir in the basil leaves, roughly shredded, and serve with the cucumber batons.

Simple Sweet Grapefruits

Serves 6

The simplest of summer starters, and one of the most delicious. Particularly ideal for large numbers of people as they are so easy to prepare.

3 pink grapefruits
6 teaspoons white sugar

Halve the fruits by cutting them across their bellies (as opposed to across the stalk end of the fruit). Using a thin serrated knife carefully cut across the exposed flesh, separating each segment. Next cut around the edge of the fruit, separating the flesh from the skin. If you have a grapefruit knife (which is serrated and curved at the end) use this, otherwise the thinner the blade the better. The trick is to get underneath the segments so each is cut away from its tethering pith. Finally, place the halves in individual bowls, sprinkle each with a teaspoon of sugar and serve.

Bruschetta

Serves 2-6
Cooking time: 3-6 minutes

Bruschetta is the Italian name for any toasted and topped bread. Use a ciabatta loaf for delicious pre-dinner snacks, easy to make over any barbecue or campfire.

1 loaf of ciabatta bread
6 oz / 150 g cherry tomatoes
6 oz / 150 g black olives, chopped
olive oil
freshly grated Parmesan cheese
salt and freshly ground black pepper

Lightly oil a square of kitchen foil and place it on the grill over hot coals or embers, reflective and oiled side uppermost (you may want to twist the edges onto the grill or secure it with some small stones to stop it blowing away). Halve the cherry tomatoes and place them on the foil. Drizzle a little oil over the tomatoes and season them as they cook with salt and fresh black pepper.

Meanwhile, slice the loaf into rounds 2 cm / 1" thick. Brush a little olive oil over both sides of each slice and place them directly on the barbecue or campfire grill. Cook them for 2-3 minutes on one side, or until the surface is a golden and slightly charred brown. Flip the slices over and as the other sides cook place the tomato halves on top. Sprinkle a handful of chopped black olives over each slice, and add a smattering of grated Parmesan (the fresh stuff is best if you can get it). After 2-3 minutes remove the ciabatta slices and serve on a large dish.

Fish and Shellfish

Fish and shellfish are, for me, the best part of a barbecue meal because they are simple, light and incredibly responsive to smoke and other flavours. Fish is also perfect for the campfire as it can be foil-wrapped with herbs and spices to make delicious little parcels. Often, fish is at its tastiest with little more done to it than the addition of lemon juice and a twist of seasoning, but I would also recommend light and fragrant marinades, spicy bastes, and the gentle smoking of steaks and shellfish by adding dried herbs to the fire during the cooking time. The main thing is not to overpower the fish with the over-enthusiastic application of anything too powerful. If designing your own marinade, always err on the side of caution.

Baked Bay Mackerel

Serves 2-4
Cooking time: 15-25 minutes

The whole bay leaves used in this dish delicately infuse the flesh. Each fish is a meal in itself, or enough for two to share.

2 whole fresh mackerel, cleaned
12 whole bay leaves
salt and freshly ground black pepper
6 tablespoons olive oil
1 lemon, sliced, to serve

Lay each mackerel on a large sheet of lightly oiled kitchen foil (shiniest side uppermost) and season well. With a sharp knife make 6 deep diagonal slits across the body of the fish, and into each slit press a whole bay leaf. Drizzle olive oil over the length of the mackerel and wrap the foil tightly around it. Cook on the grill over hot coals for 20-25 minutes, or directly in campfire embers, for 15-20 minutes, turning occasionally. Serve directly from the foil parcels, garnished with lemon slices.

Teriyaki Fish Skewers

Serves 4
Cooking time: 15-20 minutes

Teriyaki is a simple concoction of soy sauce, ginger and garlic and works spectacularly well with all meats. Tinker around with the garlic and ginger levels to suit your taste.

2 tuna steaks (approx 8 oz / 200 g each)
2 swordfish steaks (approx 8 oz / 225 g each)
1 red pepper, seeded
8 button mushrooms
2 tablespoons dark soy sauce
2 tablespoons sesame oil
2 garlic cloves, crushed
2 teaspoons fresh ginger, peeled and finely chopped
salt and freshly ground black pepper

Cut the fish steaks and the red pepper into evenly sized chunks of approximately 1 cm / ½" sides, lay them in a shallow dish with the mushrooms and season well. Combine the teriyaki ingredients, i.e. the soy, oil, garlic and ginger, and pour the mixture over the vegetables and fish. Cover and chill for 30 minutes before cooking, and if you are using bamboo skewers place them in some water to soak. Before cooking, thread the fish and vegetables onto skewers alternating tuna and swordfish, mushroom and pepper. Grill the skewers over hot coals or campfire embers for 15-20 minutes, or until the vegetables are crisp, basting occasionally and turning regularly.

Hoki Mini Tikka Kebabs with Cheater Raitha

Serves 4
Cooking time: 8-10 minutes

This raitha is a cheater because it's so easy to make – and is the perfect balance to the spiciness of cumin and coriander that infuse the fish.

for the kebabs:
4 hoki fillets
½ pint / 300 ml natural yoghurt
2 tablespoons fresh coriander, roughly chopped
1 teaspoon cumin
1 teaspoon paprika

for the raitha:
½ pint / 300 ml natural yoghurt
¼ cucumber, diced
½ teaspoon paprika

In a food processor combine the yoghurt, coriander, cumin and paprika. Do this in short bursts so the yoghurt stays smooth but the ingredients are all well combined. Cut each hoki fillet into four evenly sized chunks. Place the chunks in a bowl and pour the yoghurt mix over the top. Leave this mixture covered and chilled for at least 20 minutes. While you're waiting, soak 4 bamboo skewers in cold water for 10 minutes (you can alternatively use metal skewers, but they might be a bit big for these mini kebabs) and make the raitha. To do this simply chop the cucumber and mix it with the yoghurt, pour the lot into a serving bowl and garnish with a little paprika. When the fish has had long enough to marinate, thread the chunks onto the skewers, four chunks to a skewer. Place them on the grill over hot coals for 8-10 minutes, turning them frequently. Serve with the raitha as a cooling dip.

Prawns with Chilli, Lime and Coriander Dressing

Serves 4
Cooking time: 2-4 minutes

Prawns are unbeatable barbecue food. This recipe assumes you are using the grey, uncooked prawns, but supermarket-bought pink prawns (which have already been cooked) will work just as well, though need to be cooked for a shorter period. Just buy the biggest prawns available.

1 lb / 500 g tiger prawns
4 tablespoons lime juice
3 tablespoons fresh coriander, roughly chopped
4 tablespoons olive oil
1 large garlic glove, crushed
½ teaspoon chilli powder
1 lime, quartered, and coriander sprigs to serve

Mix together the lime juice, coriander, olive oil, garlic and chilli powder, and set aside 3 or 4 tablespoons of the resulting mixture to dress the prawns with once they're cooked.

Shell the prawns, if you need to, and tip them into the remaining mixture. Leave them to marinate for 10 minutes, then grill them for 1-2 minutes each side. Serve on a platter drizzled with the dressing you set aside earlier and garnished with lime quarters and sprigs of coriander.

Piri-piri

Serves 4
Cooking time: 4-6 minutes

Piri-piri marinade dates from Portugal's colonial days (they'd import the red hot chillies from Brazil) and can be used to spice up just about anything. It works particularly well with poultry and, in this case, scallops.

1 lb / 500 g scallops
4 dried red chillies
1 teaspoon rock salt
3 tablespoons olive oil
3 tablespoons cider vinegar

Finely chop the chillies and mix them in a bowl with all the other ingredients. Marinate the shellfish in this sauce for at least 30 minutes before cooking. Remove the scallops from the marinade and grill them over hot charcoal for 2-3 minutes each side.

Chermoula Tuna

Serves 4
Cooking time: 8-10 minutes

Chermoula is a fiery Moroccan marinade that works well with any fish, and contains the distinctively fresh, knock-out combination of cumin and coriander.

4 tuna steaks
4 tablespoons olive oil
2 large garlic cloves, crushed
1 red chilli, seeded and finely chopped
1 tablespoon fresh coriander, roughly chopped
1 teaspoon ground cumin
1 teaspoon paprika
juice and zest of 1 lemon
lemon wedges, to serve

Lay the tuna steaks in a single layer in a shallow dish. Mix together the oil, garlic, chilli, coriander, lemon juice, zest and spices and pour the mixture over the tuna, ensuring it is evenly coated. Cover and chill, preferably overnight. To cook, place the tuna directly on the grill over hot coals. Cook for 4-5 minutes on one side, then turn the steaks over and top with any remaining marinade. Grill for a further 4 minutes, test with a skewer to ensure it is thoroughly cooked (the flesh will be an even colour throughout its thickest part) and serve on a bed of couscous or with a selection of grilled vegetables.

Simple Swordfish Steak

Serves 4
Cooking time: 6-8 minutes

Swordfish can be cooked directly on the grill without fear of it falling apart. Its texture is incredible, and it is delicious with nothing more done to it before cooking than a rub with a little oil, salt and pepper.

4 swordfish steaks
1 tablespoon olive oil
crushed rock salt
freshly ground black pepper
1 lime, quartered, to serve

Rub the swordfish steaks well with rock salt, oil and black pepper. Place them directly on the grill over hot coals and cook for 3-4 minutes on each side. You can check how well cooked the steak is by piercing the middle with a skewer. As with tuna, if the flesh is darker in the centre than at the edges the steak is still rare. An even colour throughout means the fish is cooked. Serve garnished with a lime wedge and a selection of grilled vegetables.

Rosemary and Thyme Smoked Swordfish

Serves 4
Cooking time: 6-8 minutes

Thyme and a little garlic give the classic swordfish steak something extra, while the herbs leave the flesh with a delicate, smoky texture.

4 swordfish steaks
1 large garlic clove, crushed
2 tablespoons fresh thyme, chopped
3 tablespoons dried rosemary
1 tablespoon dried thyme
1 tablespoons olive oil
crushed rock salt
freshly ground black pepper

Crush the garlic into a bowl containing the oil, salt, pepper and chopped thyme. Mix together well and smear the resulting paste onto both sides of the swordfish steaks, rubbing it well into the flesh. Place the steaks directly onto the grill and cook for 3-4 minutes on each side, or until thoroughly cooked. As you cook, liberally sprinkle the dried thyme and rosemary over the coals beneath the fish.

Orange and Ginger Marinated Swordfish

Serves 2
Cooking time: 6-8 minutes

A simple marinade with an orange zing that works well with all fish, but especially tuna and, as here, swordfish.

2 swordfish steaks
zest of 1 orange
2 teaspoons fresh ginger, peeled and finely chopped
2 spring onions, finely chopped
3 tablespoons light soy sauce
3 tablespoons olive oil

Combine the spring onions, soy sauces, olive oil, ginger and orange zest in a bowl and pour the mixture over the swordfish steaks. Cover, chill and marinate the fish for at least 30 minutes, preferably 2 hours. Cook the steaks over hot coals, directly on the grill, for 3-4 minutes each side.

Salmon Fillets

Serves 4
Cooking time: 10-12 minutes

Salmon needs little augmentation as it is fresh tasting and beautifully textured in itself – but if you're looking for a little extra try it with herbs or ginger, honey and lime. Otherwise these parcels are simplicity itself.

4 boneless, skinless salmon fillets
2 tablespoons lemon juice
1 tablespoon olive oil

Lightly oil 4 squares of kitchen foil and place a salmon fillet on each. Brush lightly with lemon juice and oil and wrap the salmon in the foil, leaving space for a little air inside each foil parcel. Place on the grill over hot coals or embers for 10-12 minutes, turning once halfway through the cooking time. You'll know they're ready when white juice begins to leak from the flesh.

Herby Salmon with Sun Dried Tomato Salsa

Serves 4
Cooking time: 10-12 minutes

This salmon recipe is slightly more complicated but worth the extra effort involved. The fresh herbs produce a wonderful fragrance if you open the foil parcels at the table.

4 skinless salmon fillets
2 tablespoons olive oil
4 tablespoons lemon juice
2 tablespoons fresh tarragon, chopped
2 tablespoons fresh dill, chopped
salt and freshly ground black pepper

for the salsa
2 oz / 50 g sun-dried tomatoes
2 oz / 50 black olives, chopped
1 large garlic clove, crushed
2 tablespoons fresh basil, roughly chopped
2 tablespoons olive oil
1 tablespoon Balsamic or red wine vinegar

Oil 4 squares of kitchen foil and place a salmon fillet on each. Evenly sprinkle the tarragon and dill, olive oil and lemon juice over each fillet and season well. Fold the foil over to form parcels with a little air inside, and place them on the barbecue, or directly onto campfire embers. Cook for 10-12 minutes, turning frequently.

The salsa is worth making beforehand. Briefly whizz the tomatoes, olives, garlic and basil together in a food processor until you have a chunky mix. Stir in the vinegar and olive oil and mix well. Serve the salmon fillets and spoon salsa over the top of each.

Ginger, Lime and Honey Baked Salmon

Serves 4
Cooking time: 10-12 minutes

These salmon fillets are zesty, sweet, sour and sticky all in one parcel.

4 skinless salmon fillets
2 tablespoons runny honey
2 teaspoons fresh ginger, peeled and finely chopped
juice and zest of 2 limes
1 tablespoon olive oil
1 tablespoon vegetable oil
salt and freshly ground black pepper

Heat the vegetable oil in a frying pan over a high heat and fry the salmon fillets for 1 minute on each side, or until brown. Remove the fillets with a fish slice and lay each on a square of kitchen foil (shiniest side uppermost). Season lightly and sprinkle the ginger, a little olive oil and the lime juice over the top. Spoon the honey over the fillets to seal the ginger onto the flesh, then top with the grated lime zest. Fold the foil up to make loose parcels with some air space in them. Place the parcels on the grill over hot coals or embers for 10-12 minutes, without turning, or until the honey bubbles and thickens.

Cod Gremolata

Serves 4
Cooking time: 6-10 minutes

A zesty Italian blend of parsley, lemon and garlic – try it with chicken too.

4 boneless cod fillets
4 tablespoons olive oil
4 tablespoons fresh parsley, roughly chopped
2 large garlic cloves, crushed
juice and zest of 1 lemon
1 lemon, sliced into 8
salt and freshly ground black pepper

Arrange the cod fillets in a single layer in a shallow dish and season well. Mix together the oil, parsley, garlic, lemon juice and zest, and pour the mixture over the cod, brushing it over if necessary to ensure the fish is thoroughly coated. Cover and chill overnight. To cook, place the cod fillets on individual squares of kitchen foil, top with any remaining marinade and a slice of lemon, and wrap the foil around the cod to form parcels. Place the parcels on the grill for 8-10 minutes, turning once during the cooking time, or into hot embers for 6-8 minutes, turning often. Serve the fish directly from the parcels with the remaining lemon slices.

Baked Chatham Trout

Serves 2
Cooking time: 10-15 minutes

Flaked almonds and fish – this is a personal favourite that's so easy to cook anywhere. The light, nutty flavour makes this perfect as a romantic meal for two if served with grilled or steamed vegetables and a dollop of creamy mash. Try roasting the almond flakes for a nuttier flavour.

2 trout fillets
2 tablespoons flaked almonds
2 tablespoons olive oil
salt and freshly ground black pepper

Place the trout fillets on lightly oiled squares of kitchen foil. Lightly season the flesh and cover with a tablespoon of flaked almonds. Drizzle olive oil over each fillet and wrap in foil. As you won't be turning these, wrap the foil loosely around the fish, closing it tightly at the top to keep the air and aroma in. Grill over hot coals for 12-15 minutes, or place directly into campfire or charcoal embers for 10-12 minutes. Serve with a selection of vegetables and creamy mash.

Trout in Thai Marinade

Serves 4
Cooking time: 8–10 minutes

Variations of this marinade are widely used in south-east Asia to give fish the aromatic lemongrass and spice taste so reminiscent of the Thai coast, and with trout it tastes simply superb.

4 trout fillets
2 tablespoons fresh coriander, roughly chopped
1 stick lemongrass
2 small red chillies, seeded and finely chopped
juice and zest of 1 lime
2 teaspoons fresh ginger, peeled and finely grated
1 tablespoon light soy sauce
2 tablespoons vegetable oil

Lay the trout fillets in a shallow dish. In a separate bowl mix together the rest of the ingredients, adding the stick of lemongrass last. Spoon the mixture over the fillets, covering them completely. Cover and chill for at least 30 minutes before cooking. When thoroughly marinated remove the fillets from the dish and place them on individual squares of kitchen foil. Discard the lemongrass stick and spoon the remaining marinade over the fish, and then wrap each fillet tightly in the foil. Place the parcels on the barbecue grill over hot coals for 4-5 minutes on each side, or directly into campfire embers for 6-8 minutes in total, turning occasionally. Open the parcels at the table to let the aroma come wafting out.

Basil and Pine Sole

Serves 4
Cooking time: 12 minutes

This uses an Italian marinade designed for oven roasting that transfers perfectly to any campfire or barbecue. It uses loads of basil, but it's worth it.

4 skinless sole fillets
salt and freshly ground black pepper

for the marinade:
4 tablespoons olive oil
juice of 2 lemons
1 tablespoon fresh basil, finely chopped

for the salsa:
6 tablespoons fresh basil, roughly chopped
2 tablespoons pine kernels, roughly crushed
1 tablespoon extra virgin olive oil

Season the sole fillets and marinate them overnight in a simple mixture of oil, lemon juice and 1 tablespoon of chopped basil leaves. Just before you come to cook the fish, prepare the basil and pine salsa – whizz together the remaining basil, pine kernels and extra virgin olive oil until even but still a little lumpy. Brush a little oil over both sides of the fillets and place them directly on the grill over hot coals. Cook for 6 minutes on one side then turn them over. While the other side cooks, brush the basil and pine kernel sauce over the top, evenly coating the sole. After a further 6 minutes they're ready to serve.

Pepper and Coriander Tuna

Serves 4
Cooking time: 8-10 minutes

With their slightly hot taste these are reminiscent of peppered beef steaks, but with a lighter, crumblier texture.

4 tuna steaks
1 tablespoon black peppercorns
2 tablespoons coriander seeds
salt
1 lemon, quartered, to serve

Rub both sides of the tuna steaks with salt. Crush the peppercorns and coriander seeds together in a pestle and mortar, and press the resulting mixture evenly into both sides of the steaks. Brush with a little oil and grill over hot coals for 4-5 minutes each side. Serve immediately with freshly cut lemon wedges.

Remoulade Salsa

Serves 4

A fresh sauce, especially delicious served on grilled shellfish.

2 teaspoons capers
2 teaspoons anchovy paste
4 gherkins
1 tablespoon fresh tarragon
4 tablespoons mayonnaise
1 tablespoon Dijon mustard

Simply whizz the ingredients together in a food processor until smooth and refrigerate until needed.

Food for Carnivores

Meat is not to everyone's taste and you can easily have a successful barbecue or campfire meal without it. However, it is usually when meat on the grill begins to sizzle that borderline vegetarians begin to waver. There is something inherently satisfying about smoky, succulent chicken, crisply glazed chops and juicy, flavoursome burgers, and they are hard to resist. Meat is at its best when well marinated in herbs and spices that bring out, rather than overpower, its natural flavour and texture. It is also at its most healthy when grilled, and to the health-conscious, the sight of excess fat dripping away and vaporising on the coals is a reassuring one. I would always, in any case, choose cuts with a low fat content, and in my opinion it is worth shelling out that little bit extra for meat that has been organically reared in free-range conditions.

Mixed Grill Skewers

Serves 4
Cooking time: 12-15 minutes

Clearly both the Mummy and the Daddy of kebabs, with a potent, live and kicking marinade to boot. A proper feast for any occasion.

4 skinless and boneless chicken breasts
16 raw prawns, peeled
2 good pork sausages
1 swordfish or tuna steak
1 red pepper
1 courgette
16 button mushrooms
1 red onion
5 cloves garlic
4 spring onions, finely chopped
2 tablespoons light soy sauce
4 tablespoons olive oil
1 tablespoon fresh chives, chopped
2 small red chillies, seeded and chopped
salt and freshly ground black pepper

Make the marinade by mashing the garlic with a little salt until it forms a paste, then mixing it into the olive oil, soy sauce, chopped spring onions, chives and chillies. Season well and reserve 2 tablespoons of the mixture in a separate bowl for basting with later.

Next chop the chicken, sausages, fish, pepper and courgette into similar-sized chunks. Thread them onto 8 large, flat, metal skewers with the mushrooms and prawns, alternating vegetable-meat-vegetable or as you see fit. Place the completed skewers on a tray or on kitchen foil and pour the marinade over the top. Cover, chill and leave overnight to marinate.

To cook, transfer the skewers to a grill over hot coals or embers and cook for 12-15 minutes, or until the vegetables are slightly charred and the meat is thoroughly cooked, basting with the reserved sauce. Serve hot in briefly grilled pitta breads, or just as they are.

Poultry

Chicken, which has a habit of being a slightly bland staple indoors, comes to life on the barbecue because it is such a good absorber of flavour. So, the marinades you use will permeate the flesh while maintaining the fibrous texture that makes it such a favourite. Meanwhile, the smoky heat slightly crisps and gently flavours the outside. With all poultry dishes I can heartily recommend adding dried herbs to the fire itself towards the end of the cooking time: try sprinkling a handful of rosemary over the coals for an extra touch of smoky, herby flavour.

Chicken Kebabs

Serves 4
Cooking time: 10-15 minutes

This is as close as I can get to the purportedly secret recipe at my favourite kebab shop – like theirs these seem to take an age to cook, but they're certainly worth it.

2 large chicken breasts (or 4 smaller ones), skinless and boneless
4 tomatoes, halved
½ large red onion, cut into square chunks
1 tablespoon Dijon mustard
3 tablespoons natural yoghurt
½ teaspoon ground cardamom
½ teaspoon turmeric
½ teaspoon hot curry powder
juice of ½ a lemon

In a bowl mix together the mustard, yoghurt, lemon juice and spices. Cut the chicken into 16 even cubes and add it to the bowl. Mix until all the chicken has been evenly coated, cover the bowl and chill for at least 2 hours. Thread the chicken onto skewers interspersed with squares of onion and the tomato halves. The best skewers to use are flat, metal ones but you can use wooden ones too – just make sure you've soaked them in cold water for 10 minutes or so before you use them as this will stop them from burning.

To cook, place the kebabs on the barbecue over hot coals, turning occasionally and basting continuously with the remaining marinade (although don't baste for the last 3 minutes of cooking time). After 10-15 minutes the chicken should be tender and thoroughly cooked – serve immediately with briefly barbecued pitta bread and a fresh green salad.

Chicken Breasts with Soy, Wine and Dijon Marinade

Serves 4
Cooking time: 12-16 minutes

This mish-mash of flavours is no mismatch, and makes for a delicious, slightly sharp and distinctly Continental preparation for poultry.

4 large boneless chicken breasts (with skin)
¼ pint / 150 ml dry white wine
2 tablespoons dark soy sauce
2 tablespoons Dijon mustard
1 tablespoon lemon juice
1 dash Tabasco sauce
1 teaspoon sesame oil

Mix together the white wine, soy sauce, mustard, lemon juice, sesame oil and Tabasco in a bowl. Rinse the chicken breasts and pat them dry with paper towels, then add them to the bowl and coat them well with the marinade. Cover the surface of the chicken-marinade mix with cling film, and refrigerate for at least 2 hours (although it's best if left to chill overnight).

To cook the breasts, grill them over hot coals for 6-8 minutes each side, grilling the skin side last until it is crisp and golden. As with all chicken dishes, test with a skewer to ensure it is thoroughly cooked (the juices will run clear) and serve.

Oregano Thigh Fillets

Serves 4
Cooking time: 15-20 minutes

Thigh and leg meat has a darker colour when cooked and a more subtle texture than breast meat. Try using it in place of breast in any of the recipes if you prefer it – but do bear in mind that the irregular shape may require a slightly longer cooking time.

8 chicken thigh fillets
2 tablespoons dark soy sauce
4 tablespoons olive oil
juice of 1 lemon
6 tablespoons fresh oregano, chopped
1 garlic clove, crushed
salt and freshly ground black pepper

Mix the soy sauce, olive oil, lemon juice, oregano and garlic together in a bowl. Spoon the resulting mixture over the thigh fillets, arranged in a shallow dish. Cover and chill for at least 2 hours. To cook, place the thighs on the barbecue over hot coals and grill for 15-20 minutes, turning frequently and basting with any remaining marinade halfway through cooking.

Parsley Butter Breasts

Serves 4
Cooking time: 12-16 minutes

These are delicious – and if done right have the satisfying messiness of proper barbecue food. As the butter drips off them prepare yourself for a few little flare-ups underneath.

4 large chicken breasts (with skin)
4 oz / 100 g unsalted butter
4 tablespoons fresh parsley, roughly chopped
generous pinch of salt
freshly ground black pepper

Mash the butter and salt together until it forms a creamy paste. Add to this the chopped parsley and season well with black pepper. Smear the parsley butter under the skins of the chicken breasts, taking care not to remove the skins completely. Grill on the barbecue over hot coals for 6-8 minutes each side – grill the skin side last until it is golden and slightly crispy. Serve with crusty bread to mop up the tasty, buttery mess. It may have made a mess of your coals, but it will have been worth it.

Orange Turkey

Serves 4
Cooking time: 12-16 minutes

Turkey is a good alternative to chicken and has a lower fat content. Although turkey is slightly less resistant to absorbing flavour, in this dish its texture combines well with the citrus tang of orange.

4 turkey breast fillets
200 ml orange juice
4 tablespoons light soy sauce
4 tablespoons runny honey
2 tablespoons white wine vinegar
1 teaspoon fresh ginger, finely chopped or grated
1 teaspoon cayenne pepper
1 quartered orange, to serve

Between sheets of cling film or greaseproof paper gently flatten out the turkey breasts rolling with a rolling pin using the tips of your fingers. Lay the breasts in a single layer in a shallow dish.

Simmer together the orange juice, soy sauce, honey, vinegar, ginger and pepper in a heavy-based saucepan for 5-10 minutes, until a thick citrus aroma starts to waft out from the pan. Pour the sauce over the turkey breasts, cover them and chill until ready to cook, ideally for at least 2 hours. Grill the breasts over hot coals for 6-8 minutes each side, basting once halfway through the cooking time. Garnish with the orange quarters and serve with a green salad and buttered new potatoes.

Tandoori Grilled Chicken

Serves 4
Cooking time: 12-16 minutes

The barbecue is a reasonable approximation of the wood-fired clay ovens – or Tandoors – originally used to cook this dish, and from which it derives its name.

4 large chicken breasts, boneless and skinless
½ pint / 300 ml natural yoghurt
4 tablespoons garam masala
2 teaspoons paprika

In a bowl mix the paprika and garam masala into the yoghurt. Fill a small cup with some of the mixture and set aside. Pour the remaining mixture over the chicken breasts, arranged in a shallow dish. Refrigerate overnight, or for at least 2 hours before cooking. To cook, grill the chicken over hot coals for 6-8 minutes on each side, basting well throughout the cooking time with the reserved sauce. Serve in briefly barbecued pitta breads, and with a crisp green salad.

Peking Sticky Plum Duck

Serves 4
Cooking time: 16-20 minutes

You could use any part of the duck for this – I've chosen the breast fillets because they have the lowest fat content.

4 skinless duck breasts
4 tablespoons plum jam
1 tablespoon rice wine (e.g. Shao Xing)
1 tablespoon light soy sauce
1 garlic clove, crushed
1 red chilli, seeded and finely chopped
1 teaspoon Chinese Five Spice powder
salt and freshly ground black pepper

Combine the jam, wine, soy, garlic, chilli and Five Spice and mix together well, seasoning liberally with black pepper. Wash the breast fillets under cold water and pat them dry with kitchen towel. Place them in a shallow dish and pour the plum marinade over them, coating the breasts evenly. Cover and refrigerate for at least 2 hours before cooking. To cook, grill over hot coals or embers for 8-10 minutes each side, basting frequently with the marinade. It's good to serve up the duck with any remnants of the sticky plum sauce you have left poured over, but make sure you heat it through thoroughly first.

Marmalade Glazed Duck

Serves 4
Cooking time: 16-20 minutes

These breasts are ready in a jiffy with a glaze that seals in their natural flavours.

4 duck breasts
2 tablespoons runny honey
4 tablespoons marmalade
juice and zest of 2 oranges

Heat the honey, marmalade, orange juice and zest together in a saucepan. Bring to the boil, then simmer for 5 minutes. Brush half the mixture over the breasts, coating them evenly, and place them on the grill over hot coals or embers, skin side down for 8-10 minutes, or until the glaze and skin begin to crisp. Turn the breasts over, coat the skin side with the remaining glaze, and cook for a further 8-10 minutes. Allow the breasts to stand for 2 minutes before serving.

Teriyaki Drummers

Serves 4
Cooking time: 10-15 minutes

Teriyaki – a phenomenally simple Japanese invention, is any combination of soy, sesame, garlic and ginger, and is very tasty. If you are a garlic fiend or a ginger worshipper this is a good one to tinker around with to suit your tastes.

8 chicken or turkey drumsticks
150 ml dark soy sauce
2 tablespoons sesame oil
1 tablespoon peanut oil
2 large garlic cloves, crushed
1 tablespoon fresh ginger, finely chopped or grated

Mix together the oils, soy sauce, ginger and garlic and simply brush the mixture over your drumsticks as they cook over hot coals. Allow 10-15 minutes for the drumsticks, turning them frequently during cooking so they are evenly cooked.

Sesame Breasts

Serves 4
Cooking time: 12-16 minutes

The nutty sesame taste makes these chicken breasts decidedly oriental.

4 large skinless chicken breasts
1 tablespoon brown sugar
2 tablespoons dark soy sauce
2 tablespoons sesame seeds
2 large garlic cloves, finely chopped or crushed
freshly ground black pepper

Combine the sugar, soy sauce, sesame seeds, garlic and a liberal helping of black pepper in a shallow dish and mix together well. Add the chicken breasts and turn them to coat evenly with the marinade. Cover and chill for at least 2 hours.

Io cook, grill over hot charcoal or embers for 6-8 minutes, turn and baste well with the remaining marinade mixture and cook for a further 6 minutes.

Tequila Chicken Sunset

Serves 4
Cooking time: 12-16 minutes

So you're never drinking again? ... Right. You'd think this isn't a good recipe to cook for anyone with a hangover, unless you're feeling particularly malicious, but these sunset special kebabs are a hell of a lot tastier than you'd first think, and are mercifully also guaranteed to have zero alcohol content once cooked.

2 large skinless chicken breasts
juice and zest of 1 orange
2 tablespoons tequila
4 tablespoons olive oil
1 red pepper
1 yellow pepper
salt and freshly ground black pepper

In a bowl, mix together the tequila, orange juice, zest and oil. Cut the breasts roughly into 2 cm / 1" chunks and stir them into the tequila mixture. Add a little black pepper, cover and leave at least 2 hours for the juices to soak in – they're at their best if left overnight. When the chicken has sat in the marinade for as long as you have, core, seed and wash the peppers, and cut them also into 2 cm / 1" square-ish pieces. Thread the chicken and peppers onto 4 skewers (you choose how, and it'll depend on how much flesh you got out of the breasts. A haphazard arrangement might make a 'witty, ironic comment' . . . and anyway won't be entirely unattractive). Remember if you're using bamboo skewers to soak them in cold water for 10 minutes beforehand so they won't burn. Place the kebabs on a grill over hot coals and cook for 10-15 minutes, turning occasionally. Serve in barbecue-warmed tortilla bread, and with a fresh and spicy tomato salsa (see, for an example, the salmon fillets on page 67).

Sausages

The humble pork sausage represents a barbecue paradox: on the one hand you want the filling to be flavoured with the delights of your favourite marinade, yet on the other you know you have to prick the sausage's skin all over with a fork to allow this to happen. However, pricking the sausages before cooking really spoils them as when they grill all their delicious juices come spurting out. The best compromise – short of the tiresome and frustrating experience of making your own – is to coat them in thick sauces that become crisp when cooked, giving the sausage an exciting outer crust while maintaining its juicy core. Fortunately, a wide range of interesting sausages are available at most supermarkets, and all of those I've seen should work with these simple recipes. Always buy good quality sausages of 75 per cent pork or more, preferably with natural casings, and always ensure that they are thoroughly cooked before serving, even if this means increasing the cooking times prescribed here. Remember that a blackened sausage will not necessarily be cooked all the way through, so adjust the grill height if your bangers are cooking too quickly on the outside. You *can* test sausages with a skewer to see if the colour is consistent throughout, but the only sure-fire method I know is to slice a sample sausage in half – for all the recipes below I've added an extra sausage to the ingredients list that, if you need, you can use for this purpose.

Mustard Glazed Sausages

Serves 4
Cooking time: 12-18 minutes

This truly is simplicity itself, and will brighten the dullest of bangers.

9 good pork sausages
4 tablespoons grainy mustard
4 tablespoons brown sugar

Smear each uncooked sausage well with the grainy mustard (you can use English mustard if you want a little more kick, but use it sparingly). Dip and roll the sausages in the brown sugar until they are thoroughly coated, then grill them over hot charcoal or campfire embers immediately. Keep turning them with tongs for 12-18 minutes until they are golden, slightly crispy, and cooked throughout.

Sonya's Honey Snap Bangers

Serves 4
Cooking time: 12-18 minutes

Sonya is Australian and assures me that back home they use this recipe when no one has any money. It's pretty tasty too – a bonza budget belly-filler.

9 good pork sausages
8 tablespoons runny honey
4 tablespoons dark soy sauce

Mix together the soy sauce and honey and pour it over the sausages in a dish. Chill for at least 1 hour, then remove the sausages and grill them over hot charcoal or campfire embers, turning regularly with tongs, for 12-18 minutes or until thoroughly cooked.

Sticky Plum Sausages

Serves 4
Cooking time: 12-18 minutes

These use the same marinade as the Chinese recipe for duck fillets, only here the sauce is thicker so it clings to the sausages and forms a crust as it cooks.

9 good pork or boar sausages
6 tablespoons plum jam
1 tablespoon rice wine (e.g. Shao Xing)
1 tablespoon light soy sauce
1 teaspoon Chinese Five Spice powder
2 teaspoons corn flour
1 garlic clove, crushed
1 small red chilli, seeded and finely chopped
salt and freshly ground black pepper

Combine the jam, wine, soy, spice, garlic and chilli and season well. Stir the corn flour into a little water so it forms a smooth paste and add it to the mixture, mixing until smooth (you can use plain flour if you don't have corn flour – it won't be disastrous). Place the sausages in a dish and pour over the mixture, evenly coating them, then cover and chill until ready to cook (you don't really need a 'marinating' period, but the sauce works better if the flavours are allowed to mingle for an hour or so). To cook, place the sausages directly onto a grill over hot coals, turning regularly and basting often with the remaining plum sauce, for 12-18 minutes or until thoroughly cooked.

Dijonnaise Sausage Dip

For a simple dip, or a sauce to smear over sausages in buns, add 1 part Dijon mustard to 1 part mayonnaise. Mix lightly with a fork to give a tempting marbled effect.

Summer Mustard Dip

Combine 2 tablespoons of natural yoghurt, 2 tablespoons of Dijon mustard, 2 teaspoons of fresh, chopped dill (half that amount if using dried), and a quarter cucumber, finely chopped, to use as a light dipping sauce for sausages.

Pork and Lamb

Chops are barbecue staples: they're easy to cook and come miraculously packaged by nature with their own handles. Be wary that the flesh, which is tougher than delicate fish and poultry, is resistant to absorbing surrounding flavours, so if trying out a marinade leave the meat in it overnight in a covered dish.

Golden Glazed Pork Chops

Serves 6
Cooking time: 10-20 minutes

Honey and mustard are a classic combination – and this glaze makes the most of a simple pork chop.

6 lean pork chops
1 tablespoon English mustard (prepared)
4 tablespoons runny honey
1 teaspoon salt
1 teaspoon rosemary

Blend the mustard, honey, salt and rosemary together and smear the sauce liberally over the pork chops. Grill the chops over hot coals for 5-10 minutes each side, or until the outside is crackling and golden.

Shanghai Drunken Pork

Serves 4
Cooking time: 10-20 minutes

The rice wine gently tenderises the pork as it marinates in this traditional Chinese recipe, which also works well with chicken and fish such as fresh tuna and swordfish.

4 thick pork loin chops
4 tablespoons rice wine (or white wine)
4 tablespoons light soy sauce
4 tablespoons yellowbean sauce
2 tablespoons brown sugar
2 teaspoons fresh ginger, peeled and finely chopped

Mix together the wine, soy and yellowbean sauces with the sugar and ginger. Pour the mixture over the pork chops, laid in a shallow dish. Cover the dish and chill for at least 4 hours before cooking (preferably overnight) to allow the marinade to seep into the flesh.

To cook, remove the chops from the marinade (which you can then discard) and cook them over hot coals or embers for 5-10 minutes each side, or until cooked throughout and golden on the outside.

Four Cheese Escalopes

Serves 4
Cooking time: 14–18 minutes

Bubbling cheese should spew forth from these pork packages to tell you when they're ready. The finished result creates an impression of hours of toil – when, in fact, they're fairly easy to throw together. Perfect for showing off without trying too hard.

2 lb / 1 kg pork fillet, trimmed of excess fat
1 oz / 25 g freshly grated Parmesan cheese
1 oz / 25 g mozzarella cheese
2 oz / 50 g Gruyère cheese
2 oz / 50 g Cheddar cheese
1 teaspoon fresh sage, finely chopped
1 garlic clove, peeled
salt and freshly ground black pepper
16 cocktail sticks, soaked in cold water for 10 minutes

Try to find the thinnest, flattest fillet you can find. Cut it into 8 even pieces. Place each piece in turn between two sheets of cling film or greaseproof paper and squish each one out with a rolling pin to form a rectangular escalope. Be patient when doing this – apply firm, even pressure, but not so much that it will destroy the texture of the meat. When the meat is as thinly spread as it's going to get, season it well with salt and pepper, and rub one side of each piece with the peeled garlic clove (which you can then discard).

Next grate the Parmesan, Gruyère and Cheddar together in a bowl and add the sage and mozzarella (which is tricky to grate, so tear it into little pieces) and season well. Spoon this mixture into the centre of each piece of pork and spread it out evenly with the back of a spoon. Carefully roll the escalopes up, rolling from the shortest side of the rectangle, and secure each roll with a cocktail stick through its centre.

Cook the escalope rolls on the grill over hot coals or embers, for 14-18 minutes in total, turning regularly throughout the cooking time.

Philippine Pork

Serves 4
Cooking time: 16-20 minutes

This Philippine marinade is really intended for poultry, but its sweet and spicy orange tang gives pork that little bit of extra zing.

4 large pork chops
2 tablespoons Worcestershire sauce
2 tablespoons brown sugar
2 tablespoons orange juice
1 tablespoon light soy sauce
1 tablespoon rock salt
2 large garlic cloves, crushed
1 small red chilli, seeded and finely chopped
freshly ground black pepper

Combine the Worcestershire sauce, sugar, orange juice, soy, salt, garlic and chilli and mix well. Pour the mixture over the pork chops in a shallow dish. Cover and chill for at least 4 hours (but I'd recommend leaving it overnight if possible). To cook, place the chops on a grill above hot coals or embers for 8-10 minutes each side, basting every now and then with the remaining sauce.

Mustard Glazed Lamb

Serves 4 or 8
Cooking time: 10-20 minutes

Sugar and mustard are a wonderful combination to glaze any meat (it works brilliantly with sausages, for instance), and is one of those simple solutions to a budget constraint that's hard to beat.

8 lamb cutlets or 4 larger lamb chops
3 tablespoons English mustard (prepared)
3 tablespoons brown sugar
salt and freshly ground black pepper

Season the cutlets or chops well with salt and black pepper. Smear the mustard liberally over both sides and dip them in the brown sugar so they're evenly coated. Grill them over hot coals for 5-6 minutes each side if you're using cutlets, and 8-10 minutes for chops, which are slightly thicker. Serve immediately.

Honey and Rosemary Lamb Chops

Serves 4
Cooking time: 16-20 minutes

These chops are tasty, great to look at and ridiculously simple to prepare – an easy and impressive meal to knock up in a few minutes.

4 thick lamb chops
4 tablespoons runny honey
2 sprigs fresh rosemary
salt and freshly ground black pepper

Chop the rosemary sprigs into small sections. Season both sides of the chops and, with a sharp knife, pierce the surfaces. Into these piercings insert the chopped rosemary sprigs. Lay the chops in a shallow dish and pour the honey over the top, turning the chops over to ensure they are evenly coated.

Place the coated chops directly on the grill over hot coals or embers for 8-10 minutes each side, or until they are crackling and golden. Serve with a fresh salad.

Cheddar Chops

Serves 4
Cooking time: 17-22 minutes

A simple spread for lamb and pork chops.

4 lamb or pork chops
6 oz / 150 g Cheddar cheese
1 tablespoon Dijon mustard
breadcrumbs made from 2 slices of good crustless white bread
1 tablespoon olive oil
salt and freshly ground black pepper

Grate the Cheddar into a bowl, add the mustard, breadcrumbs and oil, season and mix well. Smear the mixture onto both sides of pork or lamb chops that have been grilled for about 16-20 minutes. Return the chops to the grill, cooking for a further 1-2 minutes on each side, or until they are a golden, crispy brown.

Ribs

Ribs are at their tastiest if marinated well so when cooked the flesh falls delicately away from the bone. Cooking ribs either requires plenty of kitchen foil and – because they can take an age to cook – your patience, or the short-cut route of parboiling them beforehand for 25-30 minutes, then chargrilling them over hot coals or embers. Remember that there's never that much flesh on a rib – so provide plenty if serving them as a main course – and that they work best if provided as sticky and sumptuous finger-food.

Chargrilled Sweet and Sour Spare Ribs

Serves 4-6
Cooking time: 15-20 minutes

The classic spare rib dish in quicksharp time – boil the ribs before you marinate them to tenderise them and reduce the grilling time.

2 lb / 1 kg spare ribs
4 tablespoons pineapple juice
2 tablespoons brown sugar
2 tablespoons runny honey
2 tablespoons lime juice
2 tablespoons concentrated tomato purée
2 small red chillies, seeded and finely chopped
2 garlic cloves, finely chopped or crushed
2 teaspoons fresh ginger, peeled and finely chopped
1 teaspoon paprika
1 red onion, finely chopped

Separate the ribs with a cleaver, if necessary (your butcher will do this for you if you ask him nicely), and add them to a large saucepan of boiling water. Simmer the ribs for 25-30 minutes, or until the flesh begins to separate slightly from the bone. Drain the ribs and leave them on kitchen towel to cool.

While the ribs are boiling away, prepare the sweet and sour sauce. Do this by heating together in a heavy saucepan the onion, garlic, ginger and chillies in a little vegetable oil over a medium heat. When the onion begins to soften (after 5 minutes or so), add the brown sugar and paprika. Continue to heat until the mixture bubbles a little. Next add the pineapple juice, honey, lime juice and tomato purée and continue to heat until the mixture bubbles and thickens. Allow this mixture to cool then add it to the ribs, laid in a shallow dish, carefully turning the ribs so that they become evenly coated.

Cook the ribs directly on the grill over hot coals or embers for 15-20 minutes, or until they are crispy and golden, turning occasionally and basting frequently with the remaining sauce.

Texan Spare Ribs

Serves 6-8
Cooking time: 60-90 minutes

These take an age to cook and aren't really suitable for the smaller, brazier-type barbecues, but they're great for campfires and larger barbecues, and they make an awesome sticky mess that's as delicious slurped off fingers as it is on the ribs themselves.

2 lb / 1 kg spare ribs
3 oz / 75 g brown sugar
1 tablespoon paprika
1 teaspoon salt
1 teaspoon English mustard powder
1 teaspoon chilli powder
½ teaspoon cayenne pepper
1 teaspoon cinnamon
2 tablespoons Worcestershire sauce
4 tablespoons white wine vinegar
6 tablespoons tomato purée
juice of 1 lemon
1 small onion, finely chopped

Prepare the marinade by mixing together all of the ingredients (except for the ribs) in a saucepan and simmering the mixture over a low heat for 10-15 minutes – this heating gives the sauce extra oomph and thickness, but isn't one hundred per cent necessary, so omit if you'd rather.

Separate the ribs with a cleaver (if necessary), lay them in a single layer on a large sheet of foil inside a lipped baking tray and pour the marinade over them. Wrap the foil around the ribs to form a big parcel, then take another, similar-sized sheet of foil and give the parcel a second wrapping – it's important to keep the juices enclosed in order for the ribs to become really tender. Chill for an hour or so, or until ready to cook.

To cook, transfer the parcel to the barbecue – if you have a large enough cooking area place it directly onto the coals at one side of the barbecue (then you can still cook other food on the grill), otherwise place it on the grill and, if you have a barbecue lid, cover. Cook for 1 – 1 ½ hours, carefully removing the parcel with oven gloves every 20 minutes to give it a quick shake, ensuring that the ribs are properly basted.

Simple Country Ribs

Serves 4-6
Cooking time: 15-20 minutes

If you don't have the luxury of time, try grilling the ribs after soaking them in this simple marinade. If you leave the ribs overnight the meat should become tender and fall away from the bone after cooking.

2 lb / 1 kg spare ribs
4 tablespoons brown sugar
4 tablespoons Worcestershire sauce
2 tablespoons lemon juice

Combine the sugar, Worcestershire sauce and lemon juice and spoon it over the separated ribs. Cover and chill overnight. To cook, grill the ribs over hot charcoal or embers for 15-20 minutes, or until the flesh is tender and starts to fall away from the bone easily, turning and basting occasionally.

Beef

Grilling over the high heat of a barbecue or campfire brings out the best in beef, sealing by searing and maintaining a juicy, pink centre. You should seal the outsides of steaks with thick flavours to complement the full taste of the flesh, and you are likely to find most cuts of beef difficult to marinate with anything but the strongest aromas.

For the average thickness of cut over hot coals, a cooking time of 3 minutes each side will be plenty for a juicy, rare steak. Allow 5 minutes a side for medium rare and, if you must, 7-8 minutes for a well done. Before serving steaks I'd recommend leaving them (called letting them 'rest') for 2 minutes to allow the juices, which will have retreated to the centre of the cut during cooking, to spread throughout the meat.

Asada Steaks

Serves 4
Cooking time: 6-16 minutes

This quick rub is the simplest way to prepare beef for barbecuing.

4 sirloin steaks
2 large cloves of garlic, crushed
2 tablespoons olive oil
crushed rock salt
freshly ground black pepper

Pat the steaks with a kitchen towel to remove any excess moisture. Rub both sides well with a mixture of crushed garlic, olive oil and rock salt and season well with black pepper. Leave the steaks covered and chill until ready to grill. Cook over hot coals until the steaks are done as you and your guests prefer. Serve with salad, potatoes and plenty of bread to mop up the juices.

Peppered Steak with Lemon Basil Salsa

Serves 4
Cooking time: 6-16 minutes

Another quick and incredibly simple preparation for steaks, served with a slightly sharp, deliciously herby salsa.

for the peppered steak:
4 sirloin or fillet steaks
2 tablespoons whole black peppercorns
1 garlic clove, peeled (but not crushed)
salt and freshly ground black pepper

for the salsa:
2 tablespoons sundried tomatoes, roughly chopped
4 tablespoons fresh basil, roughly chopped or torn
1 tablespoon fresh oregano, roughly chopped
1 tablespoon olive oil
juice of 1 lemon
salt and freshly ground black pepper

Prepare the salsa in advance by blending the herbs, oil, lemon juice, tomatoes and a little seasoning in a bowl or a food processor. If using the latter method, blend in short bursts so the consistency of the salsa remains chunky. Store the salsa in a fridge until needed.

To prepare the steaks, crush the peppercorns roughly in a pestle and mortar (or under the flat of a heavy knife). Rub the steaks with the garlic clove – which you can then discard – and season well. Press the crushed peppercorns into both sides of the steaks (they will stick best in tender, fillet steaks), then cook the steaks directly on the grill over hot coals or embers until done to your liking.

Allow the meat to rest for a minute or two, then serve topped with tablespoonfuls of the salsa.

Beef Teriyaki, Yakiniku Style

Serves 6–8
Cooking time: 4–8 minutes

Yakiniku restaurants, popular in Japan, consist of a flame grill in the centre of the seating area, on which everyone can cook their own meat, flipping it with long chopsticks. This cooking style is good for disposable barbecues on the beach, with everyone huddled around flipping the thin cuts of beef with bamboo skewers.

4 lb / 2 kg braising steak
4 tablespoons dark soy sauce
2 teaspoons sesame oil
4 large garlic cloves, crushed
4 teaspoons fresh ginger, peeled and finely chopped

Freeze the braising steaks and while they are still frozen cut them with a sharp knife into the thinnest strips you can manage (if you don't have time for this, slice the steaks without pre-freezing them – though you'll find it hard to get really thin slices and should extend the cooking time accordingly). Allow them to defrost overnight in the bottom of a fridge. Meanwhile, combine the soy sauce, oils, garlic and ginger, and save the mixture in a sealable container.

To cook, place the strips (which you must ensure have thoroughly defrosted) on a grill over hot coals. A disposable barbecue is often best for this as it will have a grill with small perforations, so the strips won't fall through. As with fondue, let your diners cook for themselves with bamboo skewers or chopsticks, and set out the teriyaki mixture in a bowl for them to dip their strips in once cooked. Depending on the thickness of the strips, the beef will take 2-4 minutes to cook through on each side – they are ready when no pink colour in the meat remains. Dip the strips in the teriyaki sauce and eat immediately.

Red Wine, Chilli and Garlic Steaks

Serves 4
Cooking time: 6-16 minutes

Red wine permeates the thick flesh of beef better than anything else. I'd advise buying a halfway decent bottle of wine, if only so you can drink some while you do the preparation.

4 large sirloin steaks
half bottle of red wine
2 tablespoons olive oil
2 red chillies, seeded and finely chopped
2 large garlic cloves, crushed
1 tablespoon sesame seeds (optional)
salt and freshly ground black pepper

Season the steaks with salt and black pepper and lay them in a shallow dish. Combine the wine, oil, chillies, garlic and sesame seeds and pour the mixture over the steaks – add more wine to cover the meat if necessary. Cover and chill overnight to allow the flavour to penetrate. Grill the steaks over hot coals until done to your liking.

Argentinian Barbecue Baste

Serves 4
Cooking time: 16–20 minutes

You can make this garlic-based baste and marinate well in advance – its potency increases the longer you leave it, and it can be stored for up to two weeks. It works best if dolloped onto T-bones or sirloin steaks while they cook.

8 large garlic cloves, crushed
4 tablespoons olive oil
2 tablespoons white wine vinegar
2 tablespoons fresh parsley, roughly chopped
2 tablespoons fresh oregano, finely chopped, or 1 tablespoon dried oregano
1 tablespoons dried red chillies, chopped
salt and freshly ground black pepper

Simply mix all the ingredients together and store, refrigerated, in a sealed jar for at least 12 hours before use. Baste steaks with the sauce before and during cooking.

For a milder sauce, substitute the chillies for chopped, dried peppers or sun-dried tomatoes.

Fagiottini

Serves 4
Cooking time: 8-10 minutes

Get all adventurous on your guests with these delightful Milanese treats, which, despite the posh name, are simply cabbage leaves stuffed with mince.

1 large savoy cabbage
9 oz / 250 g lean beef mince
1 medium free range egg
3 tablespoons freshly grated Parmesan cheese
pinch of nutmeg
8 chives, to tie

Pull off and discard the cabbage's outer leaves. Carefully separate 8 of the inner leaves – they should be the biggest ones you can find. In a pan of boiling water blanch the leaves, i.e. dip them into the water for 1-2 minutes, and dry them on clean kitchen towels or paper. Next, mix the egg into the mince, add the cheese and no more than a pinch of nutmeg, and mix well. Lay the dried leaves on squares of lightly oiled kitchen foil (shinier side inwards) and spoon a little of the mince mixture into the centre of each leaf. For each leaf, fold up its ends then tuck over the leaf's sides, and secure each parcel with a chive tied around its middle (admittedly this is the fiddly bit, but it looks wonderful when presented). Wrap the foil around the cabbage parcels and add them to the barbecue, grilling them over hot coals for 8-10 minutes, or for 5-7 minutes in embers, regularly and carefully turning the parcels. Serve unwrapped (but not untied) and watch your artistic efforts disappear in a few mouthfuls.

Bootiful Burgers

Burgers are a crowd-pleaser, a barbecue must-have. Until you've witnessed a juicy burger dribbling into a bearded chin the barbecue hasn't really started. They are also exceptionally easy to prepare, and ridiculously easy to experiment with. All you need is some minced meat and a little imagination and you can come up with some great – and crazily great – ideas. I've given you a few here to get started, but I'm sure you can come up with some of your own.

These recipes are all designed to make four quarter-pound burgers, but feel free to make two half-pounders if you wish (just allow longer cooking times), to double up the ingredients if cooking for more people, or to substitute animal meat for vegetarian mince. If using frozen mince, make sure it's thoroughly defrosted beforehand, and make sure you roll up your sleeves and get properly messy.

The Basic Burger

Serves 4
Cooking time: 10-12 minutes

Really simple. Use good quality meat and you'll find basic is beautiful.

1 lb / 500 g lean beef mince
salt and freshly ground black pepper

Simply mix the meat well with liberal quantities of salt and pepper. In your hands divide the mixture into four equal balls, and squish each ball flat to make a burger shape. Brush each with a little oil and cook for 5-6 minutes on each side. Serve in rolls lightly toasted on the barbecue – and with plenty of pickles and tomato ketchup.

Greek Bifteki

Serves 4
Cooking time: 12-16 minutes

The Greek original has cheese sandwiched between two thin burgers. This barbecue variation has a Feta surprise in the middle.

1 lb / 500 g lean beef mince
8 oz / 225 g Feta cheese
salt and freshly ground black pepper

Mix the beef and seasoning as you would for the Basic Burger. Form it into four evenly sized balls. Now chop the Feta cheese into four even cubes and push them into the top of each ball, pressing them down until they are about in the centre. Fold the meat over to enclose the cheese. Flatten the balls down into burger shapes, brush them lightly with oil and grill over hot coals for 6-8 minutes on each side.

Cheesy Burgers

Serves 4
Cooking time: 12-16 minutes

Another cheesy surprise hidden in the middle of these super-smooth burgers.

1 lb / 500 g lean beef mince
8 oz / 225 g blue cheese (e.g. Dolcelatte or Gorgonzola)
breadcrumbs made from 2 slices of good crustless white bread
1 medium free range egg
100 ml milk
1 tablespoon fresh basil, chopped
1 tablespoon fresh oregano, chopped

Combine the mince, breadcrumbs, egg, milk and herbs and mix well but not to a pulp, then form four evenly sized balls from the mixture. Cut the cheese into even cubes and press each cube into the heart of the ball, as you would with the Bifteki (above). Fold the meat over and enclose the cheese. Press the balls down into burger shapes, brush them with oil and grill for 6-8 minutes on each side.

Kamikaze Burgers

Serves 4
Cooking time: 10-12 minutes

Wasabi novices may wish to tread carefully before committing barbecue seppuku – the unassuming green paste is like supercharged horseradish.

1 lb / 500 g lean beef mince
1 tablespoon fresh ginger, finely chopped
1 tablespoon dark soy sauce
4 teaspoons wasabi paste
salt and freshly ground black pepper

Make the burgers by blending the beef with the seasoning, and adding the chopped ginger and soy sauce. Divide the mixture into 4 even balls. With your thumbs or a spoon make an indentation in the top of each ball, so the ball becomes a bowl. Make up the wasabi paste according to the packet instructions (it often comes as a green powder and is prepared similarly to mustard, but you can buy it ready-made) and spoon a solitary teaspoon of the paste into each cavity. Close the lip of the 'bowl' over the paste and flatten the burger down, so you have a beef and ginger outer enclosing a wasabi nucleus. Grill over hot coals or embers for 5-6 minutes on each side. Serve with plenty of cooling liquid to hand!

Stuffed Wigan Burgers

Serves 4
Cooking time: 12-16 minutes

This Northern classic saves you putting tomato ketchup on your burger.

1 lb / 500 g chuck steak mince
1 small green chilli, seeded and finely chopped
1 tablespoon olive oil
salt and freshly ground black pepper
1 tablespoon English mustard (prepared)
1 tablespoon tomato ketchup
1 dash Tabasco sauce
2 oz / 50 g medium Cheddar cheese

First make the burgers by combining the beef, chilli, olive oil and seasoning together in a bowl. When thoroughly mixed, form 4 evenly sized balls. Place them on a tray, but don't press them down into burgers just yet. Instead make indentations with your thumbs or a spoon at the top of the ball so they form small bowls. Now mix together the mustard, ketchup and Tabasco in a separate bowl and grate in the cheese. Spoon this mixture into the burger cavities and push the meat together at the top, sealing in the mixture. Flatten down the balls to form burger shapes, brush lightly with oil and grill over hot coals for 6-8 minutes each side. Serve in buns with relish and fresh salad.

Thai Burgers

Serves 4
Cooking time: 10-12 minutes

With fragrant lemongrass for a taste of Thailand.

1 lb / 500 g lean beef mince
1 shallot or small onion, finely chopped
1 tablespoon lemongrass, finely chopped
1 red chilli, seeded and finely chopped
4 tablespoons unsalted peanuts, crushed
1 tablespoon olive oil
salt and freshly ground black pepper

Mix the shallot, lemongrass, chilli, peanuts and oil together in a bowl (or briefly whizz them in a food processor until you have a rough and lumpy consistency). Add the beef mince, season, and mix until the peanut and spice are evenly distributed throughout the meat. Form them into 4 evenly sized balls, squish the balls down to form burgers, oil them lightly and cook over hot coals for 5-6 minutes each side.

Pork and Thyme Burgers

Serves 4
Cooking time: 10-12 minutes

The leaner and lighter meat of pork is more susceptible than the usual beef mince to the spices and gentle fragrances included in this mixture.

1 lb / 500 g lean pork mince
½ medium onion, finely chopped
1 small garlic clove, crushed
2 tablespoons fresh thyme, chopped
1 tablespoon olive oil
salt and freshly ground black pepper

Simply mix all the ingredients together and season well. Divide the mixture into four balls, flatten the balls into burger shapes, brush with a little oil and grill over hot coals for 5-6 minutes each side. Serve with a good tomato relish in lightly toasted buns.

Spicy Pork and Coriander Burgers

Serves 4
Cooking time: 10-12 minutes

Served with peanut sauce, these burgers are the missing link between Bangkok and the local chip shop.

1 lb / 500 g lean pork mince
½ red onion, finely chopped
2 tablespoons fresh coriander, roughly chopped
1 small red chilli, seeded and finely chopped
1 large garlic clove, crushed
2 teaspoons ginger, peeled and finely chopped
1 tablespoon vegetable oil

Prepare and cook in exactly the same way as the Pork and Thyme burgers.

Excellent with a spicy peanut sauce, made by combining 2 tablespoons of crunchy peanut butter, 2 teaspoons of sweet chilli sauce, 2 tablespoons of dark soy sauce and ½ a teaspoon of cumin. Spoon the sauce over the cooked burgers.

Westbourne Lamb Burgers

Serves 4
Cooking time: 12-16 minutes

The invention of these burgers (by throwing everything into a bowl) was one of those random cooking experiences that somehow seemed to work, although by rights it shouldn't have.

1 lb / 500 g lamb mince
1 red onion, finely chopped
1 large garlic clove, crushed
2 tablespoons fresh mint, chopped
2 teaspoons dried mixed herbs
½ teaspoon cumin
½ teaspoon cayenne pepper
1 medium free range egg
1 tablespoon olive oil
salt and freshly ground black pepper

Combine all the ingredients together in a bowl – there's really no need to beat the egg first – and mix them together well, seasoning the mixture generously. Divide the mixture into four balls, squish them flat, brush with a little oil and grill for 6-8 minutes each side. Serve with a crisp green salad and a little (ready-made or home-made) mint sauce.

Kafta

Serves 4
Cooking time: 10 minutes

The original Lebanese burger-kebab.

1 lb / 500 g lamb mince
½ onion, finely chopped
2 large garlic cloves, crushed
3 tablespoons fresh mint, chopped
2 tablespoons fresh parsley, roughly chopped
1 teaspoon cumin
½ teaspoon coriander seeds, ground
1 teaspoon salt
freshly ground black pepper

Combine all the ingredients in a bowl and mix well. Using your fingers, form balls about the size of an egg from the mixture. Thread a skewer through each ball and mould the mixture into a long finger along the length of the skewer. Lightly oil the meat and grill for 10 minutes, turning occasionally. Traditionally, these are served wrapped inside square pitta breads (you can make these by cutting a square from a normal pitta), briefly heated on the grill, with chopped tomatoes, cucumber, lettuce and natural yoghurt.

Food for Vegetarians

In my experience, vegetarians always seem to get a bit of a raw deal at barbecues – the problem is not so much that they can't be catered for, more that hosts tend to forget (unless they are vegetarians themselves), and so inevitably one ends up with the ubiquitous leek and cheese quaterpounder, pulled from the murkiest recess of the deep-freeze and grilled on the barbecue's loneliest corner. My advice, even to the most hardened of carnivores, is to try a chargrilled courgette or asparagus spear: you'll experience a delicate shudder as your heart and preconceptions melt. The best thing about barbecuing vegetables, aside from the fabulous taste, is the diversity – and the following recipes will provide side dishes to main courses, or can be mixed to form spectacular and colourful vegetarian platters. Do remember that true vegetarians will object most strongly to their food being grilled on fatty, meaty grill residue, so if you're pressed for space you could consider a couple of disposable barbecues dedicated to cooking veggie dishes and sides.

Halloumi and Mixed Pepper Kebabs with Basil Oil

Serves 4
Cooking time: 10-15 minutes

There's something distinctly Mediterranean about red, yellow and orange peppers – so much so that the introduction of a single green slice can radically change the feel of this dish. The brightly coloured reds, yellows and oranges are also the sweetest and work the best on the grill.

12 oz / 300 g Halloumi cheese
2 red peppers
1 orange pepper
1 yellow pepper
6 tablespoons olive oil
4 tablespoons fresh basil, chopped
salt and freshly ground black pepper

Core, seed and wash the peppers, and chop roughly into 2 cm / 1" squares (though don't get the ruler out – they'll look great whatever you do with them). Similarly, chop the cheese into 2 cm / 1" cubes. Thread the cheese and peppers onto flat metal skewers (for this kebab recipe I'd really advise against using bamboo skewers, which have the habit of turning themselves and not the food – the cubes of cheese swing and are a hassle to turn individually), and season well. You can experiment here with combinations of colour – you'll have to be truly aesthetically challenged to make this lot look unappealing.

Before you start cooking, prepare the basil oil. Do this simply by blending the basil and oil together in a food processor on its speediest setting until you are left with a smooth green liquid.

Place the kebabs on the grill over hot coals and cook them for 10-15 minutes (or until the peppers develop that roasted, charred look), basting them constantly with the basil oil. Serve in a briefly barbecued pitta bread with a fresh green salad and natural yoghurt, or simply serve them on a dish, garnished with the remaining oil and a sprig of basil, and let everyone dig in.

New Potato Skewers with Rosemary Oil

Serves 4
Cooking time: 10-15 minutes

Make sure your potatoes get the point with these tasty, sizzling skewers. For extra flavour, try using a handful of rosemary sprigs (if you have plenty to hand) instead of your trusty basting brush.

for the skewers:
2 lb / 1 kg new potatoes
1 tablespoon olive oil
1 tablespoon unsalted butter
salt and freshly ground black pepper

for the oil:
2 tablespoons rosemary leaves
4 tablespoons olive oil

Boil the potatoes before barbecuing, having washed them first, in a large saucepan of boiling water for 10-15 minutes (or until they are tender).

Meanwhile, make the rosemary oil. Do this by simply blending the rosemary and olive oil in a food processor at a high speed until you have a smooth consistency and even colour.

Drain the potatoes, and in the saucepan toss them with the seasoning, butter and remaining olive oil. When they are cool enough to handle, halve the potatoes and thread them onto flat metal kebab skewers, or bamboo skewers that have been soaked in cold water for 10 minutes beforehand.

Place the potato kebabs on the grill over hot coals or embers for 10-15 minutes, or until golden brown and charred in places, basting regularly with the rosemary oil.

Vegetable and Herb Kebabs

Serves 4
Cooking time: 15-20 minutes

These skewers are simple to prepare and cook. The listed ingredients are only a suggestion – experiment away with different combinations of vegetable.

2 aubergines
2 red peppers
16 button mushrooms
16 cherry tomatoes
1 celery stalk
8 small onions
juice and zest of 1 lemon
2 tablespoons olive oil
2 garlic gloves, crushed
2 tablespoons fresh thyme, chopped
2 tablespoons fresh basil, chopped
2 teaspoons dried oregano
salt and freshly ground black pepper

First wash all the vegetables well. Cut the aubergines, red peppers and celery into evenly sized chunks (about 2 cm / 1" cubes in the case of the aubergines, 2 cm / 1" slices for the celery and peppers). Peel the onions, remove the stalks from the tomatoes and thread all the vegetables onto skewers in the most attractive combination of colour you can muster. Place the skewers on a large dish and drizzle over them the mixture of olive oil, lemon juice and zest, garlic and thyme. Cover and chill for an hour or so.

Just before you come to cook the skewers, roll them in a mixture of salt, pepper, basil and oregano, then place them directly on a grill over hot charcoal or embers. Cook for 15-20 minutes, or until the vegetables are tender and slightly crispy, turning frequently and basting with a little olive oil.

Stuffed Mushrooms

Serves 4
Cooking time: 8-10 minutes

If you can find mushrooms large enough, these cheesy delights will make a meal in themselves – otherwise serve them as an accompaniment to vegetable kebabs or meat dishes.

8 large flat mushrooms
2 slices good white bread, crusts removed
2 oz / 50 g mature Cheddar cheese
1 tablespoon fresh thyme, chopped
1 tablespoon fresh oregano, chopped
1 tablespoon fresh basil, chopped
1 garlic clove, crushed
olive oil
salt and freshly ground black pepper

Wash the mushrooms and remove their stems. Place the stems in a food processor with the herbs, bread, garlic, seasoning, cheese and a tiny drizzle of olive oil. Blend in short bursts to produce an even mixture with a rough texture. Brush the brown undersides of the mushroom caps with oil and place them on the grill over hot coals or embers and cook, underside-down, for 4-5 minutes. Brush the mushroom tops with oil and turn over. Fill the now exposed bowl of the mushroom undersides with the cheese, crumb and herb mixture. Cook for a further 4-5 minutes, or until the cheese begins to melt, and serve immediately.

Feta and Vegetable Roastie

Serves 4-6
Cooking time: 45 minutes

A delicious and filling main course, or a tasty side to meat dishes. Easy to cook and, when the foil parcel is ripped open at the table, an eye-catching centrepiece.

2 lb / 1 kg courgettes
1 lb / 500 g tomatoes
8 oz / 225 g Feta cheese
2 red peppers, cored and seeded
2 red onions, finely chopped
2 tablespoons black olives
2 tablespoons fresh thyme, chopped
2 tablespoons olive oil
1 tablespoon balsamic vinegar
salt and freshly ground black pepper

Chop the courgettes into wheels and the peppers into rough 2 cm / 1" squares and place them on a large sheet of kitchen foil, folded double for strength. Add the chopped onion, thyme, seasoning and drizzle well with oil. Wrap into a parcel, sealing with a flap at one end so that it will be easy to add the remaining ingredients. Seal, shake well and add the package to barbecue or campfire embers. Cook for 30 minutes, shaking the package occasionally to mix the ingredients. Meanwhile, skin the tomatoes by standing them in freshly boiled water for 1 minute then chop them into chunks. Cut the Feta into cubes, and roughly chop the olives.

When ready, remove the package from the embers and (carefully!) open the sealed flap. Add the tomatoes, olives, cheese and balsamic vinegar. Reseal, shake well and return the package to the embers for a further 15 minutes.

Serve straight from the foil package.

Bootiful Veggie Burgers

The preconception of veggie burgers being wholesome yet bland stodge is a little misguided. As health-consciousness reaches new heights the humble vegetable concoction is enjoying something of a renaissance. No doubt if you are a vegetarian you will have already encountered the principle dilemma facing veggie burger chefs: should one produce something that looks like its animal cousin, or an entirely outlandish design that is a burger only in name? I don't expect these recipes will help resolve the dispute, but you might have fun trying them out.

Remember, vegans, that most vegetarian mince brands will contain reconstituted egg and are therefore not suitable for you to use.

The Original Veggie Burger

Serves 4
Cooking time: 10-15 minutes

*Experienced vegetarian chefs will undoubtedly take issue
with this recipe as everyone has their own favourite mix.
Nonetheless, this blend should produce a base to which
you can add herbs, spices, and a touch of Tabasco zing,
as you see fit. Leave out the coriander and ginger for a
milder taste.*

8 oz / 225 g floury potatoes, peeled and chopped
2 large carrots, peeled and finely chopped
½ white cauliflower, chopped
2 oz / 50 g frozen peas, defrosted
2 oz / 50 g green beans
2 tablespoons fresh coriander, chopped
1 red onion, finely chopped
2 large garlic cloves, crushed
1 teaspoon fresh ginger, peeled and finely chopped
2 tablespoons milk
2 tablespoons unsalted butter
½ teaspoon cumin
small pinch of nutmeg
1 large free range egg
salt and freshly ground black pepper

Boil the potatoes and carrots until tender enough to mash
(20-30 minutes). Meanwhile, steam the cauliflower, peas
and beans for 10-15 minutes. Drain the vegetables and
mash them together with half the butter, milk, a pinch of
nutmeg and liberal seasoning. Next, fry the onion and
garlic in the remaining butter until soft. Stir in the coriander
and cumin and add this mixture to the vegetable mash.
   Finally, crack and mix in the egg, and with lightly floured

hands form 8 even balls from the mixture, which you can then flatten down on greaseproof paper to form burger shapes. Grill the burgers over hot coals or embers for 10-15 minutes, or until evenly brown and crispy, turning occasionally and carefully, and basting with a little olive oil.

Red Tofu Burgers

Serves 4
Cooking time: 5-15 minutes

Colourful, sweet, and suitable for vegans.

1 lb / 500 g tofu
6 oz / 150 g oatmeal or porridge oats.
4 tablespoons fresh basil, chopped
4 tablespoons fresh oregano, chopped
3 tablespoons brown sugar
1 tablespoon paprika
1 teaspoon cumin
salt and freshly ground black pepper

In a large bowl, combine the tofu and the oats. Keep stirring and add more oats if necessary – the consistency you need is such that the mixture becomes difficult to stir, but not so dry that it crumbles. Add the herbs, spices and seasoning, stir well, then with lightly floured hands gently form the mixture into 8 evenly sized balls. Place these on greaseproof paper and press them down into burger shapes. Wrap each burger in lightly oiled kitchen foil and place on the barbecue grill for 10-15 minutes, or directly into campfire embers for 5-10 minutes, turning occasionally.

Nutty Burgers

Serves 2-4
Cooking time: 10-15 minutes

When cooking with nuts it's sensible to warn your guests, just in case of nut allergies. These burgers are not masquerading as the real meat McCoy, though, as the nuts have a taste and texture all of their own.

2 oz / 50 g fresh white breadcrumbs
1 oz / 25 g pecan nuts
8 oz / 225 g mushrooms, sliced
1 large potato, peeled
1 red pepper, chopped
1 medium onion, finely chopped
2 garlic cloves, crushed
1 small green chilli, seeded and finely chopped
2 tablespoons hoi sin sauce
1 tablespoon unsalted butter
1 tablespoon olive oil
salt and freshly ground black pepper

In a heavy frying pan, fry the pecan nuts in a little oil over a medium heat until they start to go brown. Drain them on a kitchen towel then grind them in a food processor or pestle and mortar, and set aside to cool. Next, fry the onion and garlic together in the butter and oil over a medium heat until the onion begins to go soft and brown. Grate the potato into the pan, add the chopped red pepper, chilli and mushrooms and cook for a further 10-15 minutes. Mix in the hoi sin sauce, and continue to cook until the sauce thickens and bubbles. Transfer the mixture to a food processor and blend it together with the pecan nuts and breadcrumbs in short bursts so the mixture retains a rough consistency. Season well and chill the mixture in a covered dish to allow it to firm up. After about an hour's chilling time, form the mixture into four evenly sized balls. Press them flat on greaseproof paper to form burger shapes, brush with a little oil and grill them over hot coals or embers for 10-15 minutes, turning carefully halfway through the cooking time.

Brighton Belles

Serves 4
Cooking time: 10–12 minutes

A delightful and slightly hot Albion of egg, bread and veggie mince. Best served by the sea.

1 lb / 500 g vegetarian mince
1 medium free range egg
breadcrumbs made from 2 slices of good crustless white bread
2 teaspoons English mustard (prepared)
1 tablespoon Worcestershire sauce
1 tablespoon olive oil
salt and freshly ground black pepper

Mix all the ingredients together in a bowl. Be sure to season well, and when the ingredients are combined, form the mixture into four even balls. Squish each one down to make a burger shape, brush with oil and cook over hot coals for 5-6 minutes each side.

Toasted Spinach and Ricotta Burgers

Serves 4
Cooking time: 4 minutes

A British invention with Italian soft cheese. These are best served as browned patties, crisp on the outside yet deliciously moist in the centre.

8 oz / 225 g ricotta cheese
8 oz / 225 g fresh spinach
4 slices good white bread, crusts removed
pinch of nutmeg
1 medium free range egg, beaten
ciabatta bread, to serve

Wash the spinach and remove any larger stems. Steam over boiling water for 3-4 minutes, until the spinach begins to wilt and reduce in size. Leave it to cool and drain.

Place the breadcrumbs in a bowl and spoon in the ricotta. With a squeeze of your hands, remove any excess moisture from the spinach and add it and the nutmeg to the bowl. Mix the cheese, breadcrumbs and spinach together well, adding the egg and continuing to stir until the mixture binds. Form four small balls from the mixture and press them flat to form thin patties.

Brush the burgers lightly with oil and grill them over hot coals for 2 minutes each side, or until the cheese and breadcrumbs begin to crisp and char slightly. At the same time place 8 thin slices of ciabatta loaf, brushed lightly with oil, on the grill until they begin to turn brown. Serve the burgers sandwiched between the ciabatta slices.

Summer Salads

The barbecue salad should be light, unpretentious and colourful – avoid faffing around arranging leaves into geometric designs and carving roses from carrots, and instead prepare something aching to be heaped onto a plate. They should also, however, be incredibly tasty and satisfyingly fresh, so always use the best ingredients available, and let your dressings speak for themselves. All of the salads I've listed here could rightfully exist as meals in themselves, but crisp salads are the perfect accompaniment to barbecued food and in the summer they come into their own. Use them as a guide, though, not a rule, and experiment with colour and taste to your heart's content.

Simple Green Salad with Cheese and Chive Dressing

Serves 4-6

The classic green salad is simple and perfect – everything green, heaped in a bowl, delicately coated with a fresh, cheesy sauce. Its simplicity and crispiness, though, means it goes well with just about any dressing, so feel free to experiment.

for the salad:
1 small lettuce
½ cucumber, halved and sliced
1 green pepper, seeded and sliced
1 bunch of watercress
4 spring onions, finely chopped
1 celery stick, chopped
1 head of chicory, chopped
3 tablespoons fresh thyme, chopped
2 tablespoons fresh marjoram, chopped

for the dressing:
2 oz / 50 g Stilton cheese
2 oz / 50 g Roquefort cheese
2 oz / 50 g low fat cream cheese
6 oz / 150 g natural yoghurt
1 tablespoon mayonnaise
2 tablespoons chives, chopped
salt and freshly ground black pepper
cress, to serve

As the salad itself is easy to assemble, make the dressing first. With a fork, mash the cheeses together in a bowl, then gradually stir in the mayonnaise and yoghurt until smooth and creamy. Season with salt and pepper to taste, stir in the chives, and leave the whole lot to chill until ready to serve. To assemble the salad start with the biggest pieces first so that the smaller pieces don't get hidden at the bottom before you serve it. Tear the lettuce leaves into the bowl, add the pepper, cucumber and watercress, then the celery, chicory and spring onions. Finally, top with a generous helping of the dressing, a sprinkle of watercress, and serve.

Avocado and Bacon Salad

Serves 6-8

Avocado and bacon is as desperately unhealthy as a salad will ever get, so make sure you trim those rinds. This is a classic, though, and it is delicious. Do remember that uncooked egg, contained in the dressing, is unsuitable for either pregnant women or the elderly.

for the salad:
8 rashers of rindless streaky bacon
8 large lettuce leaves (Lollo Rosso or iceberg)
1 bunch watercress
2 ripe avocados
juice of 1 lemon
fresh, washed basil leaves to serve

for the dressing:
2 tablespoons white wine vinegar
6 tablespoons extra virgin olive oil
1 tablespoon Dijon mustard
1 medium free range egg yolk
salt and freshly ground black pepper

Barbecue or grill the bacon until crisp, then cut it into rough 1 cm / ½" pieces. As it cools, tear the lettuce into small pieces and arrange on a large serving dish, topping it with the cress. De-stone the avocados and roughly cut the flesh into chunks – the best way to go about this is to cut the avocado in half and scoop out the stone with a teaspoon. If the avocado is truly ripe you should be able to push the flesh out into a bowl by gently turning the skin inside out. Immediately toss the avocado chunks with the lemon juice so they are evenly coated to prevent their discolouring.

Scatter the avocado and bacon bits over the salad leaves and top with the dressing, simply made by briskly whisking together vinegar, olive oil, mustard, an egg yolk, salt and pepper. Finally, garnish with fresh basil leaves and serve.

Tabbouleh

Serves 6

Bulgur wheat is also known as Pourgouri or cracked wheat, and, like its recipe, Tabbouleh, originates from the Middle East. It makes for an excellent accompaniment to meat and poultry dishes, but be warned – substitute fresh mint for the dried kind at your own peril!

6 oz / 150 g bulgur wheat
2 tomatoes
½ cucumber
6 tablespoons fresh mint, chopped
4 tablespoons fresh parsley, roughly chopped
1 finely chopped small onion
5 tablespoons olive oil
juice of 2 lemons
salt and freshly ground black pepper
fresh mint leaves to serve

Place the wheat in a large saucepan of cold water – bring it to the boil and simmer for 15 minutes. Drain in a colander, tip the contents out into a clean, dry tea towel and allow it to cool. Gathering the edges of the towel, squeeze gently to get rid of the excess moisture, then spread the wheat evenly on a baking tray to allow it to dry further.

Peel the tomatoes (by immersing them in freshly boiled water for a minute or so), cut them into quarters, remove the seeds and chop the remaining flesh into rough chunks.

In a salad bowl mix together the wheat, tomatoes, onion, cucumber, mint and parsley, season well and finally add the lemon juice. Serve garnished with the fresh mint leaves.

Mediterranean Feta Salad with Herb and Caper Dressing

Serves 4-6

Feta has a delicate texture and is smoothly refreshing to the palette, complementing the capers' delightful acidy tang.

for the salad:
1 iceberg lettuce, chopped
2 carrots, cut into matchstick-sized batons
1 tablespoon capers
6 oz / 150 g cubed Feta cheese
2 slices white bread, with crusts removed and cut into 1 cm / ½" cubes
sunflower oil

for the dressing:
1 tablespoon extra virgin olive oil
1 teaspoon red wine vinegar
1 tablespoon lemon juice
1 tablespoon capers
1 oz / 25 g watercress
1 large garlic clove, crushed
1 tablespoon chives, chopped
1 tablespoon fresh parsley, roughly chopped

First make the croutons. Simply fry the bread cubes in a little hot sunflower oil until golden, and immediately drain on a little kitchen towel. Next, toss together the lettuce, carrots and capers in a large bowl. Mix in the croutons and cubed Feta cheese. Make the dressing by blending all the dressing ingredients together in a food processor and pour over the salad.

Mozzarella Salad with Honey and Mustard Dressing

Serves 4-6

This dressing gives a little pizzazz to an Italian classic – but tomato and mozzarella will work just as well if simply drizzled with a little extra virgin olive oil and balsamic vinegar. It's best to get good quality mozzarella – low fat varieties, for instance, just aren't the same – and although this is a salad in name, it's at its most effective and appetising if served as a starter.

for the salad:
8 oz / 225 g Buffalo Mozzarella cheese
3 large tomatoes
3 spring onions, chopped
fresh basil leaves, to serve

for the dressing:
6 tablespoons extra virgin olive oil
juice of 1 lime
1 large garlic clove, crushed
2 teaspoons runny honey
1 teaspoon French mustard
2 tablespoons fresh basil, chopped
1 tablespoon fresh parsley, roughly chopped

Slice the cheese and tomatoes and arrange them on a large serving dish with the spring onions sprinkled over the top. Combine the dressing ingredients together and drizzle them over the salad. This dish is at its best if dressed and allowed to chill for 15 minutes in the fridge, and should be removed at least 5 minutes before it is served, garnished with fresh basil leaves.

Rocket and Fennel Salad

Serves 2-4

*A simply dressed, slightly spicy and deliciously fresh salad
with a gentle fragrance of aniseed.*

1 fennel bulb, finely chopped
2 oz / 50 g rocket
1 tablespoon black olives
2 tablespoons fresh basil, roughly torn or chopped
1 red chilli, seeded and finely chopped
4 tablespoons extra virgin olive oil
juice of 1 lemon
salt and freshly ground black pepper

Mix the rocket, fennel, olives and basil together in a bowl.
Simply dress with the lemon juice, olive oil and seasoning,
toss well, and serve, sprinkled with a scattering of red
chilli.

Sides and Snacks

Roast Garlic and Cream Cheese

Serves 4-6
Cooking time: 30-40 minutes

A simple and impressive snack, ideal as a starter or a side dish, but not advised to be eaten before a visit to the dentist.

1 whole head of garlic
6 oz / 150 g cream cheese
1 tablespoon olive oil
bread, to serve

Leaving the garlic bulb unpeeled, slice the top one eighth away from the stem end to reveal the cloves. Place the head on a square of kitchen foil and drizzle the olive oil over it. Wrap the foil tightly around the garlic and place it directly into the embers of the fire or barbecue. Cook it for 30-40 minutes, by which time the garlic inside should be soft and mushy. Squeeze it out onto hunks of fresh bread and top with the cream cheese.

Roasted Onions

Serves 4
Cooking time: 45 minutes

Onions are simply fabulous roasted – it doesn't matter what sort of onion you use, although you may find red onions require a slightly longer cooking time. Be patient and the result will be soft, translucent and utterly delicious.

4 large onions
4 tablespoons olive oil
salt and freshly ground black pepper

Top, tail and peel the onions. Using a spoon or a small knife dig some of the core away to form a well in the top of each onion. Into these wells pour the olive oil, rubbing any over-spill over the onions. Season each onion well and wrap in kitchen foil with the shiniest side facing inwards. Place them on a barbecue grill for 45 minutes, turning occasionally, or directly into the embers of a campfire for 30 40 minutes.

Garlic and Herb Mushrooms

Serves 4-6
Cooking time: 15-25 minutes

These mushrooms make a great accompaniment to just about anything.

1 lb / 500 g mushrooms
2 tablespoons olive oil
2 tablespoons unsalted butter
1 tablespoon fresh parsley, roughly chopped
1 tablespoon fresh coriander, roughly chopped
4 garlic cloves, crushed
juice of 1 lemon

Lay a large square of kitchen foil on a flat surface and lightly oil it. Place the washed mushrooms in the centre and sprinkle the chopped herbs and crushed garlic over the top. Drizzle over the olive oil and break the butter into small pieces, distributing it evenly amongst the mushrooms. Wrap the mushrooms in the foil to form a parcel and place it directly into campfire embers for 15-20 minutes, taking it out to shake the bag occasionally to mix the ingredients, or onto a barbecue grill for 20-25 minutes, turning now and then. To serve, open the parcel up and squeeze the lemon juice over the mushrooms.

Grilled Asparagus with Lemon Dip

Serves 4-6
Cooking time: 3-4 minutes

These spears are multi-purpose: they make for a great starter, side dish or as part of a vegetarian platter.

1 lb / 500 g asparagus spears
2 tablespoons olive oil
salt and freshly ground black pepper
4 tablespoons mayonnaise
juice and grated rind of 1 lemon

Rub or brush the asparagus with oil and season well. Place the spears directly on the grill over hot coals or embers and cook for 3-4 minutes, turning occasionally so they're evenly crisp and tender. Serve arranged around a small serving bowl containing mayonnaise mixed with the lemon juice and rind, and allow everyone to help themselves.

Chargrilled Lemon Courgettes

Serves 6
Cooking time: 3-5 minutes

Courgettes, which have little flavour of their own, are perfect for whacking on the barbecue or campfire grill as they act as a sponge for surrounding flavours. Experiment with throwing dried herbs (such as rosemary) onto the heat underneath them for an added, subtle fragrance.

1 lb / 500 g courgettes
2 oz / 50 g unsalted butter
juice of 1 lemon
2 tablespoons fresh parsley, roughly chopped
1 tablespoon olive oil
salt and freshly ground black pepper

Wash the courgettes, top and tail them and slice them in half lengthways (i.e. so they are long semi-cylindrical batons). Steam them for 5 minutes, then drain them well. Next, melt the oil in a large pan and add the butter. When it begins to fizzle add the courgettes, then the parsley and lemon juice. Stir to ensure the courgettes are evenly coated and then pour the whole lot into a dish, seasoning well. Transfer the courgettes from their dish to a grill and cook over hot coals for 3-5 minutes, turning regularly and basting with the butter mixture while they cook. When the flesh side is a crispy golden brown they're ready to serve.

Plantain Crisps

Serves 4-6

This Ghanaian recipe makes an unusual but tasty treat.

4 firm plantains
2 tablespoons lemon juice
4 teaspoons ground ginger
4 teaspoons cayenne pepper
2 tablespoons vegetable oil

Peel the plantains (under running water to avoid staining your fingers), slice them into rounds 1 cm / ½" thick, and sprinkle lemon juice over the pieces. In a separate bowl, combine the ginger and the cayenne pepper. Heat the oil in a heavy frying pan over a high heat. Coat the plantain pieces in the ginger and pepper mixture, then fry them in batches until they are crisp and golden. Drain the crisps on kitchen towel and serve – they're at their best hot, but are still great cool.

Garlic and Herb Bread

Serves 4-6
Cooking time: 15-25 minutes

A classic barbecue-baked baguette is a must, but if you have to, you can cheat and put it in the oven at 200ºC / 400ºF for 20 minutes. Otherwise, a top tip is to slice the loaf in half and make two foil parcels.

1 French loaf
1 tablespoon fresh parsley, roughly chopped
1 tablespoon unsalted butter
3 large garlic cloves, crushed
salt

Mash the garlic with a little salt to form a paste and mix it into softened, unsalted butter with the chopped parsley. Make diagonal slices along the length of the baguette, taking care not to chop it all the way through, and smear the butter mix into the slices. Wrap the baguette in lightly oiled foil and place it directly into campfire embers for 15-20 minutes, on a barbecue grill for 20-25 minutes. It'll be ready to serve when the butter has all melted into the loaf, it is heated through, and the crust has darkened to a deep brown.

Baked Potatoes

You could spend a whole, soul-destroying afternoon waiting for potatoes to bake on a barbecue, and it is an exercise I'd wholly advise against. For campfires, however, they are perfect as the cooking can begin almost as soon as the fire gets going. Rub a little oil into the skin, wrap them in foil, shiniest side inwards, and place them in the fire. The average potato will take 1 hour to cook – test it with a skewer to see if it's tender all the way through – and should be served with little more than salt, pepper and a little butter as a great accompaniment to all dishes.

A barbecue solution is to bake potatoes in the usual manner the day or morning before. Either re-heat them in foil on the barbecue for 20-30 minutes or, as I prefer, halve them and cross hatch the exposed flesh with a knife. Brush the surface with melted butter or olive oil, season well, and place them face down on the grill for 10 minutes, or until the surface is a golden brown, slightly charred in places. Again serve with butter, seasoning and the juiciest food you can muster.

Roasted Sandwiches

No kidding, these are delicious. Make a big sandwich using any sort of bread, wrap it in lightly oiled foil and add it to campfire or barbecue embers for 15-20 minutes. The best fillings are ones that cook as they heat. My favourite is a mixture of red Leicester, Cheddar, red onion and mango chutney, safely ensconced in the belly of a whole Grande Rustique loaf. But good old cheese and pickle works just as well – try it and see.

Gruyère Rösti

Serves 4-6
Cooking time: 16-20 minutes

This traditional Swiss dish is perfect for a barbecue or campfire meal. Make it beforehand, cut it into slices and re-heat it over hot coals when needed.

8 oz / 225 g Gruyère cheese (or mature Cheddar)
3 lb / 1 ½ kg Desiree potatoes
2 tablespoons fresh parsley, roughly chopped
2 oz / 50 g unsalted butter
1 tablespoon olive oil
salt and freshly ground black pepper

Boil the potatoes in lightly salted water for 10 minutes – after this time they should be easy to skin. Grab them with oven gloves and let the skin slide off. When cool enough, grate the skinned potatoes into a large bowl, season well and mix in the parsley.

Heat 1 oz of butter and ½ a tablespoon of olive oil together in a heavy-based frying pan until the butter starts to fizzle. Add half the potato mix, pressing it down with a spatula so it fills the whole pan evenly. Grate the cheese over the surface while it cooks, and cover the cheese with the remaining potatoes, again spreading the mix out evenly. Fry like this for 8-10 minutes over a medium heat, testing with a spatula to see if the underside has gone a golden brown.

Now comes the tricky bit: place a large plate, serving side down, over the top of the frying pan and carefully flip the contents out onto it – the rösti should come out whole, though it's not a disaster if you break it a little. Heat the remaining butter and oil in the pan and slide the rösti back on top of it, uncooked side down. Fry for a further 8-10 minutes.

Flip the rösti out onto a wire rack and allow it to drain and cool. Once cooled, cut it into eighths and refrigerate in a sealed container. To serve as a barbecue side dish, brush both sides of the slices with a little oil and place them on the grill above hot coals for 2-3 minutes each side. Works wonderfully with salad, fish and poultry.

Gypsy Toast

Serves 4-6
Cooking time: 4-6 minutes

I'm sure I've absolutely no idea why it's called that, but you might know it better as plain old eggy bread. Simple to make, this is a campfire classic.

4 medium free range eggs
a little milk
nutmeg
salt and freshly ground black pepper
8 slices of thick white bread

Lightly beat the eggs with a splash of milk, salt and pepper and, if you want a bit of extra spice, a tiny pinch of nutmeg. Meanwhile, heat some oil in a pan over hot coals (if you don't have one with you it doesn't matter – you can put the bread directly onto a lightly oiled grill). Place two slices of bread in the bowl with the beaten eggs (I prefer mine with the crusts chopped off) and allow them to soak up as much egg as they can. Remove them with a fish slice and let any excess egg drip off, then lay them, two at a time, in the hot oil (or on the grill). After about 2-3 minutes they'll be ready to turn over, with the underside a golden brown. Flip them and cook the other side for a similar length of time. Repeat the process until there's no more egg mix ... and then make some more! In camping tradition, serve with beans, grated cheese, sausages and brown sauce for a hearty start to any day.

Breakfast Tortilla

Serves 2-4
Cooking time: 7-9 minutes

A perfect campfire wake-up call. This tortilla can be cooked in advance, refrigerated and re-heated when needed. Provides all the calories needed for when you go a-wandering along a mountain-top.

4 good pork sausages, finely sliced
4 oz / 100 g button mushrooms
1 red onion, finely chopped
2 medium potatoes, peeled
1 large tin baked beans
6 large free range eggs
2 tablespoons vegetable oil

Heat the oil in a large heavy-based frying pan and add the chopped onion, the potatoes, either grated or finely chopped, the mushrooms and the sliced sausages. Cook over a medium heat, or over hot embers, for 5-7 minutes, or until the sausages are thoroughly cooked and the potatoes beginning to brown. Meanwhile, drain the beans from their juice and lightly beat the eggs. Pour both onto the potato and sausage mixture and cook until set.

Either brown the top under a grill if indoors, or flip the tortilla over onto greaseproof paper and return to the pan with a little more oil to cook for a further 2 minutes. Serve sliced into wedges. If re-heating, cook in slices on a grill over hot embers for 2-3 minutes each side, or until heated through thoroughly.

Sweetcorn

What would a barbecue be without sweetcorn? Traditionally the last thing to be ready and the most eagerly anticipated, corn-on-the-cob epitomises the truly messy, delicious, finger-licking nature of outdoor food. Get it wrapped and ready early and stuff your foil parcels on wherever they'll fit and you'll find corn to be a difficult side dish to mess up, or chargrill your corn for a darker, nuttier taste. The two most sage pieces of wisdom I can offer are these: Firstly, always chop the whole cobs in half, crossways, to form two smaller cobs. They won't cook any quicker, but they'll be easier to find room for, both on your fire and on your plate. Secondly, if you don't have any of those special cob-holding forks, then rushing out and buying some immediately would seem like folly. A better option would be to use the sharp, pointy ends of bamboo skewers (which are ridiculously cheap), hacked off with a sharp knife and a pair of scissors. Your guests will thank you for your ingenuity in solving the toothpick problem, too.

The following ideas, to get you started, assume you are cooking two ears of corn (i.e. when halved, enough for four people). Remember that cooking on the embers or directly on the coals will make the corn a little tougher and crispier (but just as good) than the slower baking of the grill. Always serve with a little butter from which your guests can help themselves.

Classic Corn-on-the-Cob

Brush ears of corn with a little melted butter, season well and wrap them in foil. Add them to the barbecue wherever you can find a bit of space, or directly to the campfire embers. Turn them occasionally and they'll be ready in

20-30 minutes on the grill, or 10-15 minutes if cooked on the coals or embers.

Chargrilled Corn

Place the ears directly on the barbecue or campfire grill. As they cook, season lightly and brush with a little melted butter or olive oil. When the ears are thoroughly brown (and slightly charred) remove them and drizzle with freshly squeezed lemon juice. Eat immediately.

Spicy Garlic Corn

Mash a peeled, crushed garlic clove with a little salt to form a paste and mix it into a generous knob of softened, unsalted butter with a heaped teaspoon of chilli powder. Smear the ears with the mixture, wrap them tightly in foil, shiniest side inwards, and cook on the grill, on coals, or in campfire embers, turning occasionally. They'll take 20-30 minutes on the grill, 10-15 minutes if cooked on the embers.

Coriander Butter Corn

Mix two tablespoons of fresh, chopped coriander into a generous knob of softened, unsalted butter. Add 1 teaspoon of ground cumin, mix well and smear the mixture over the ears. Wrap the corn tightly in foil, shiniest side inwards, and cook on the grill or directly on coals or embers until tender – 20-30 minutes on the grill, 10-15 minutes in the embers.

Corn-on-the-Cob for Cheats and Scoundrels

So, you're too lazy and impatient to do it the hard way. Worse still, your barbecue is overflowing with all those swordfish steaks and mixed grill kebabs. Simple solution: pre-boil sweetcorn for 6-8 minutes in unsalted water. Dry off the corn with kitchen towel, then prepare it as with the above recipes. As the corn is already cooked through all the barbecue will need to do is re-heat it. Cook for 5-10 minutes, turning occasionally, serve and watch everyone swoon over your speed and efficiency.

Desserts

The ideal barbecue dessert should be moist, reassuringly mushy and cooling, but with enough spice and oomph to intrigue the palette into wanting seconds. For the recipes requiring heating, remember that your sausagey, beefy grill will probably want cleaning before you cook a delicate peach on it.

Sweet Rum Plantains

Serves 4
Cooking time: 15-20 minutes

A traditional Jamaican recipe that is simple to prepare. Plantains have a firmer texture than bananas and will not become as mushy when cooked. They're delicious with this alarmingly good dressing of sugar and rum.

4 plantains
4 teaspoons brown sugar
4 tablespoons dark rum

Slit the plantains along their lengths, but keep them in their skins. Wrap each in foil and add them to campfire embers or the grill for 15-20 minutes, turning occasionally. Unwrap the plantains carefully and make a second slit along the skins parallel with the first, so you have a flap of skin you can pull away to expose the fruit underneath. Serve in bowls, sprinkled with brown sugar and a generous splash of dark rum.

Baked Honey and Lemon Apples

Serves 4
Cooking time: 30-50 minutes

Apples take a long time to cook so if you're making them on the barbecue or campfire you'd best get them on early. I assure you they'll be worth the wait.

4 large cooking apples
2 tablespoons runny honey
juice of 2 lemons
rind grated from 1 lemon
1 tablespoon sunflower oil

Leaving the apples whole, remove their cores. Wash, dry, and place each apple on a square of kitchen foil large enough to wrap it tightly. In a bowl, mix together the honey, lemon juice, rind and oil. Spoon the mixture into the apple core cavities and wrap the foil around each apple. Wrap a second piece of foil round each – this will help keep the juices in during cooking. Transfer to the barbecue: if cooking on the grill section you'll need to turn them regularly and cook for at least 50 minutes. If cooking them directly in the embers of the barbecue or campfire leave them for 30-40 minutes, turning occasionally. Unwrap the parcels carefully and serve with custard or ice cream. The apples can be cooked in a conventional oven too – follow the same procedure but fill the cavities with the honey and lemon mix while the apples sit in a baking tray: there's no need to wrap them. Bake them for 45 minutes in an oven pre-heated to 180°C / 350°F.

Iced Oranges

Serves 6

These orange sorbets, stuffed inside orange skins, are highly impressive and are above all else light, refreshing and tasty. A delicious dessert for a baking hot day.

5 oz / 125 g granulated sugar
juice of 1 lemon
12 large oranges
8 fresh bay leaves, to serve

In a heavy-based saucepan bring the sugar, half the lemon juice and 120 ml of water to the boil. After 2 minutes or so you should have a clear syrup – leave it in the saucepan, turn the heat off and put to one side.

Next, slice the tops off 6 of the oranges. You should cut only the top quarter of the stem end away. Carefully scoop the flesh of the oranges out into a bowl – but don't throw the empty orange skins and lids away as you'll need them later: freeze them in a Tupperware box until the sorbet is ready.

Grate the rind of the remaining 6 oranges into the sugar syrup. Squeeze their juice into a bowl, and add the juice from the scooped-out flesh of the decapitated oranges – it's easiest just to sieve it. This should give you a little over 1 pint / 600 ml of orange juice, but if you don't have enough, top it up with a little bought orange juice, or the juice of another orange. Pour the juice into the syrup and add 100 ml more water (about 6 tablespoons) and the remainder of the lemon juice. Taste the mixture – if it's on the tart side add a little more sugar and mix well, if it's too sweet add a little lemon juice for balance.

When it is to your liking pour the mixture into a freezer container (e.g. a large Tupperware box) and freeze for 3 hours. After this time, remove the sorbet and mix it thoroughly in a bowl to destroy the forming ice crystals. Freeze it for a further 4 hours, checking on it from time to time: the consistency you're aiming for is firm, but not solid.

When ready, spoon the sorbet into the frozen orange shells and set the lids on top. Freeze them until ready to serve. For a final touch, use a skewer to make a hole in the top of each lid. Thread a bay leaf into each to make a feather in an impressive cap.

Fruity Cinnamon Kebabs

Serves 4
Cooking time: 6-8 minutes

*This recipe will, of course, work with just about any fruit.
For a taste of the exotic try it with figs or mangoes.*

1 pineapple
2 pears
2 nectarines
8 large strawberries
2 tablespoons runny honey
2 teaspoons ground cinnamon
juice and zest of 1 orange

Prepare the fruit by peeling and coring the pears and pineapple, removing the stones from the nectarines and hulling the strawberries. Leave the strawberries whole but cut the rest of the fruit into evenly sized chunks. Thread the fruit chunks onto 8 pre-soaked bamboo (or 4 larger, metal) skewers, alternating fruits as you see fit.

In a small bowl mix together the orange juice and zest, cinnamon and honey. Place the fruit skewers on a grill over hot coals or embers and cook them for 6-8 minutes, turning frequently and basting generously with the honey, orange and cinnamon mix. Serve with cream, ice cream or just on their own.

Baked Passion Bananas

Serves 4
Cooking time: 5–15 minutes

These bananas have an incredible flavour and an even better aroma – with Grand Marnier for an extra bit of oomph.

4 bananas
2 passion fruits
8 tablespoons orange juice (freshly squeezed is best)
4 tablespoons Grand Marnier liqueur

Peel the bananas and discard the skins. Place each on a square of kitchen foil large enough to form a parcel. Halve the passion fruits and squeeze the juice and flesh (pips and all) equally over the bananas, then sprinkle 2 tablespoons of orange juice and 1 tablespoon of Grand Marnier over each. Fold the foil over to form parcels and place them on the barbecue for 10-15 minutes, or directly into the embers of the barbecue or campfire for 5-10 minutes. Unwrap the banana parcels at the table to let the aroma waft out, and serve with thick cream or ice cream.

Chocolate Bananas

Serves 4
Cooking time: 5-15 minutes

The campfire classic – bananas, mushily baked in their skins, covered in delicious dark chocolate. Incredibly simple and frighteningly addictive.

4 bananas
8 oz / 225 g dark / plain chocolate

Slice the banana skins open along their lengths (but don't peel them), and stuff lumps of chocolate in between the skin and the fruit. Wrap each banana tightly in foil to re-close the opening, and place them on the barbecue grill for 10-15 minutes, or directly into the campfire embers for 5-10 minutes, by which time the banana should be soft and the chocolate molten. Unwrap carefully and eat immediately, straight out of the skin.

Baked Pears

Serves 4
Cooking time: 20–40 minutes

Pears, like apples, seem to take an age to cook, but they work best if baked, rather than grilled, as they soften delightfully.

4 ripe pears (any variety)
4 tablespoons crème fraîche
1 tablespoon icing sugar
juice and zest of 1 orange

Peel and core the pears and wrap them in foil. Cook them on the barbecue grill for 30-40 minutes, or directly in campfire embers for 20-30 minutes. In the meantime mix together the crème fraîche, orange juice and icing sugar. Serve the pears in bowls with this creamy, orangey mixture spooned over the top, garnished with a sprinkling of the orange zest.

Strawberry Syllabub

Serves 4-6

Summer without strawberries would be like Wimbledon without valiant British defeats at the hands of more capable opponents. Even if there's nothing else to celebrate this year, celebrate the syllabub – refreshing, smooth, creamy, tasty ... and ridiculously easy to make.

1 lb / 500 g strawberries
2 tablespoons icing sugar
3 oz / 75 g caster sugar
¼ pint / 150 ml sweet white dessert wine
½ pint / 300 ml double cream
10 amaretti biscuits

Wash and then hull the strawberries (i.e. remove the green bits) and purée half of them in a food processor (if you don't have one you could mash them through a sieve). Mix the icing sugar into the purée and leave to chill.

Next whisk the sweet wine, the cream and the caster sugar together until the mixture forms soft peaks – be prepared to err on the side of caution here as you don't want to over-whip and have the ingredients separate. Transfer this mixture to a large serving dish and spoon the strawberry purée mixture over the top. Lightly swirl the two together with a fork to give a marbled effect.

Finally, halve the remaining strawberries and arrange them on top. Roughly crush the amaretti biscuits and sprinkle them over the finished dessert.

Stuffed Blackberry Nectarines

Serves 4 or 8
Cooking time: 10-20 minutes

Nectarines have the perfect consistency for a barbecue or campfire dessert with their fibrous yet bakeable mushiness. Serving them up with a good dollop of crème fraîche is a must-try experience.

4 large nectarines
2 oz / 50 g fresh blackberries
4 tablespoons brown sugar
4 tablespoons lemon juice

Wash and halve the nectarines and remove the stones. Place both halves of each nectarine on its own piece of foil, large enough to enclose the whole nectarine in a parcel. Fill the cavities with blackberries and sprinkle both the blackberries and flesh with brown sugar and lemon juice. Push the nectarine halves together (so they look like whole nectarines again, only with a sweet blackberry filling instead of a stone) and wrap them tightly in the foil. Cook on the grill above hot coals for 15-20 minutes, turning halfway through the cooking time, or directly in the embers for 10-15 minutes, turning occasionally. Serve with lashings of ice cream.

Roasted Honey Peaches

Serves 6
Cooking time: 10 minutes

Like nectarines, peaches maintain their basic shape and flavour when baked or, as in this case, grilled, yet become delicately tender and delicious to slurp down with something crunchy like the biscuit mix in this recipe.

6 large peaches
2 tablespoons almonds
4 crushed amaretti biscuits
4 tablespoons clear runny honey
1 teaspoon ground ginger

Halve the peaches and remove the stones. Place them on the grill above hot coals, cavity side uppermost. While they cook, brush a mixture of 1 tablespoon of honey and the ground ginger on the exposed flesh. After 5 minutes turn the peaches over. While the other side cooks, roughly crush or blend the almonds and amaretti biscuits and mix the remaining honey into them. After 5 minutes the peaches should be ready – slightly crisp on the outsides with the flesh soft and a little gooey. Transfer them to serving bowls, and into each cavity add a dollop of the biscuit, nut and honey mix. Simple, quick and delicious.

Honey Butter Pineapple

Serves 8
Cooking time: 5-10 minutes

I've heard this recipe called Calypso Pineapple – probably because it puts you in mind of waves lapping gently at a sun-bleached shore, but perhaps also because of what happens if you leave the rum bottle lying around.

1 large ripe pineapple
4 tablespoons runny honey
2 oz / 50 g brown sugar
2 oz / 50 g unsalted butter
6 tablespoons dark rum

Core the pineapple and cut the flesh into 8 equal wedges – you can leave the skin on if you like, and in fact you should if these are to be eaten without cutlery.

In a saucepan (you can either do this beforehand, or on the barbecue), combine the honey, butter, rum and sugar and simmer until the sauce starts to thicken. Brush the pineapple wedges liberally with the sauce and grill them over hot coals or embers for 5-10 minutes, or until the surface of the fruit is an even brown, turning them occasionally. Serve straight away, preferably with a delicious vanilla ice cream.

Crumbly Delight

Serves 4

If you're strapped for cash and ideas this makes for a cheap and surprisingly good dessert.

2 packets butterscotch Angel Delight (or similar instant dessert mix)
1 pint milk, or as per dessert packet instructions
1 pack hazelnut and chocolate chip cookies

Make the instant dessert with the milk as per the instructions on the packet. Crush the biscuits with a wooden spoon and divide the crumbly result equally between 4 bowls or for as many people as you have. Pour the dessert mix over each and refrigerate until ready to serve. For extra gourmet kudos grate a little milk chocolate over the top of each bowl.

Drinks

Proper refreshment is, of course, nearly as important an element at a barbecue as the food. If you're hosting a large party it's worth asking your guests to bring their own booze (which they're likely to anyway, suspecting you might not have enough), but it's also a good idea to have a few tricks up your sleeve and to create drinks a little more interesting than cola and squash for anyone abstaining from alcohol. It is important to remember that people dehydrate easily in the summer if sat around outdoors, especially if drinking alcohol, so wherever you are remember to set out plenty of water. And, as if it needs to be said, be safe and sensible – if you're driving simply don't drink alcohol at all.

The Devils

Simple Mojito

Serves 1

Minty fresh – but certainly not to everyone's liking – the Mojito is a wonderful summer cooler.

5 fresh, washed mint leaves
1 teaspoon caster sugar
50 ml Havana club rum (or another light rum)
1 lime
6 ice cubes, crushed
soda water

Pour the rum, sugar and mint into a hi-ball glass (or one that holds about 500 ml). Juice the lime and add both the juice and the remaining squeezed-out segments. Add the crushed ice, and swirl the contents of the glass about. Top up with soda water and serve immediately.

Cuba Libra

Serves 4

This special mix will get you all fired up for Revolution. Or you might talk about it for a bit, anyway, while you wait for those veggie sausages to cook …

350 ml rum
850 ml coke
300 ml lime juice (approximately 6 limes' worth)
12 ice cubes
lime wedges to serve

Simply combine the rum, coke, lime juice and ice together in a pitcher and mix well. Serve with lumps of ice in hi-ball glasses with wedges of lime.

Frozen Margarita

Serves 4

Not too many of these now or you'll forget all about cooking and your friends will find you later face-down in the herbaceous border, muttering to yourself.

150 ml lime juice (approximately 3 limes' worth)
1 ½ teaspoons caster sugar
275 ml tequila
150 ml triple sec
24 ice cubes, crushed
sea salt and lime to serve

In a food processor whizz the crushed ice, sugar, tequila, lime juice and triple sec together. Serve immediately in margarita glasses (if you have them – otherwise improvise) with wedges of lime. For the professional touch, frost the lip of the glass with salt by wetting the rim with a lime wedge then dipping the glass upside-down in a shallow dish of sea salt before you pour in the drink.

Strawberry Daiquiri

Serves 4

Easy to make and an incredibly fresh taste of summer in every glass, as well as a fair old whack of rum and tequila.

12 oz / 300 g strawberries
juice of 2 limes
150 ml light rum
100 ml tequila
2 teaspoons caster sugar
12 ice cubes, crushed
4 strawberries, to serve

Hull the strawberries and put them in a food processor. Add the lime juice, rum, tequila, sugar and crushed ice, whack the lid on firmly and blend until smooth. Serve immediately and professionally with a strawberry into which you have cut a groove at the tip and stuck on the rim of each glass.

Raspberry Bellini

Serves 4

This variation on the classic champagne cocktail uses a kick of brandy and raspberries, but you can experiment with other fruits. Great combinations are the traditional peach, exotic mango, and fresh summery strawberry.

8 oz / 225 g raspberries
100 ml good brandy
1 bottle champagne

Wash the raspberries and purée them in a food processor. Force the pulp through a sieve to take out any lumps and pour a little of the sieved purée into four champagne flutes. Add a shot of brandy to each glass and top up with chilled champagne. Garnish each glass with a fresh washed raspberry and serve.

The Angels

Iced Tea

A really refreshing summer cooler.

Make a large pot of tea in the usual manner, only use double the amount of leaves or tea bags. When brewed, strain the tea or remove the bags and allow it to cool. Pour it into a large jug over plenty of ice, lemon slices and, if you like it a little lighter and more sweet, a large glass of orange juice.

Strawberry and Banana Smoothie

Serves 4

Simple, satisfying, smooth.

12 oz / 300 g strawberries
1 banana
1 pint / 600 ml natural yoghurt

Wash and hull the strawberries, peel and chop the banana and place the lot in a food processor with the yoghurt. Blend until smooth, chill well and serve with lumps of ice.

Kiwi, Grapefruit and Honey Smoothie

Serves 4

Sharp and sweet, grapefruits are a perfect palette cleaner. White grapefruits will work just as well, but the pink variety give this drink a wonderful colour.

3 kiwi fruit
2 pink or red grapefruits
2 tablespoons runny honey
1 pint / 600 ml natural yoghurt

Halve the kiwis and scoop out the flesh, seeds and all (you may find it easier, if the kiwis are hard, to peel them with a sharp knife and chop the flesh). Halve the grapefruits and using a sharp, thin knife separate the segments from the skin. Pour the grapefruit segments into a food processor with the kiwi fruit, and pour in any of the remaining juice, removing the pips. Add the honey and yoghurt and blend it all together until smooth. Chill well and serve with lumps of ice.

Other cookery books
from Summersdale:

Beginner's Grub

by Alastair Williams

Beginner's Grub is designed to introduce people of all ages to the kitchen, show them around that somewhat unfamiliar room and transform them with minimal pain into competent cooks.

Alastair Williams makes cooking enjoyable with his simple yet delicious recipes interspersed with witty anecdotes. Guaranteed to impress.

£4.99 Paperback

Student Grub

by Alastair Williams

A new and updated edition of the bestselling student recipe book. Containing a wide selection of popular and easy to prepare recipes - laid-back, witty and user-friendly instructions, this is an informal guide to food and drink by a former student who knows what students like to eat and are capable of cooking.

Main meals for one or for entire households, favourite foreign dishes, all basics of cooking explained, large vegetarian section, cheap and healthy eating, dinner parties and booze-ups - everything a student needs to know and more.

£4.99 Paperback

Student Veggie Grub

by Alastair Williams

So you're a veggie - but are you bored with your two-veg? Rather than another supermarket nut cutlet, do you reach for the chips? Would you rather use tofu to grout tiles than form a staple part of your diet?

Then you need this book. With the assurance of a fulfilling culinary life and with these delicious and desirable dishes, even your non-veggie friends will agree that your food is not an 'alternative' but the most appealing option.

From practical advice on a healthy diet to encouragement in wicked indulgence, from quick and easy, and meat-free versions of everyone's favourites to dinner party impressive, this book licks the platter clean.

£4.99 Paperback

For a current catalogue and a full listing of
Summersdale books, visit our website:

www.summersdale.com